Killer Cop Antoinette Frank

Pete Dove

Published by Trellis Publishing, 2021.

While every precaution has been taken in the preparation of this book, the publisher assumes no responsibility for errors or omissions, or for damages resulting from the use of the information contained herein.

KILLER COP ANTOINETTE FRANK

First edition. July 1, 2021.

ISBN: 979-8224840656

Written by Pete Dove.

KILLER COP

THE TRUE STORY OF ANTOINETTE FRANK

PETE DOVE

Who do you trust? A doctor. A teacher. A police officer? There is something bizarrely discomforting about crime committed by those in authority. It should not really be so surprising, though, that even those in positions of power still err; after all, behind the suit, or the white coat or the badge is a human being. One with the same passions, strengths and weaknesses as anybody else.

But, somehow, we expect more from these people. And so, we feel a greater let down when they act in ways that disappoint. Add to that, when one of their victims is little more than a child, and the other a cop, any lingering sympathy that might exist for the culprit is swept away.

Antoinette Renee Frank was born in April 1971. Home wasn't the greatest of places. Her brother was on the run from the law and, even worse, her father was abusive. Although he was out of her life for long periods, when he was about he could be sexually, mentally and physically aggressive towards her.

But despite the tough upbringing she endured, Frank retained a dream – that of becoming a police officer. At the age of twenty two, it seemed as though that desire would be met. In 1993, she applied to the New Orleans Police Department to join the force. Initially, though, the dream was to be put on hold. Several indicators arose through the recruitment process which suggested she was not the kind of person the NOPD really wanted on their staff.

She was described as being 'shallow and superficial' by the psychiatrist who interviewed her. She was discovered to have lied on several occasions on her application form, including about her mental state and she failed two psychiatric tests that formed a part of the selection process. But during the 1990s New Orleans was crying out for police officers.

Poor pay meant that many good officers were finding better salaries and safer work in other fields. Corruption – including drug related crimes – was rife and the reputation of the department was at a deep low. Recruitment drives were failing to deliver results. Not least, the out-moded restriction that required all members of the force to actually be resident in the city meant that the pool of potential police officers was limited more than it might have been. On top of this, Franks possessed two characteristics which made her an attractive proposition for shortfalls which needed to be addressed and boxes that had to be ticked. Firstly, she was a female. Secondly, and more importantly, she was black.

Racial tensions in the southern City were at a particular high back in the early 1990s, and those in charge of the city's law enforcement programmes felt that by hiring officers of colour, some of that friction between the black community and the police could be eased.

So when Antoinette applied to join the force a second time, shortly after her first rejection, she was successful. She spent a month at the police academy and by the end of February 1993 New Orleans had a new and very enthusiastic officer ready to don the uniform.

Although Antoinette performed well at the academy, qualifying near the top of her class, more senior officers quickly identified some concerns regarding her performance once in post. She was seen as very quiet – shy almost. Many thought that she was too reticent and withdrawn to become an effective cop.

Then again, for a young black woman to join the white male dominated New Orleans Police Department of the early 1990s must have been a threatening and daunting task. Especially for a woman who was barely more than a child herself, and who had grown up as a victim of male abuse. The conclusion of her colleagues was that she needed more training. Concerns were expressed about the irrationality of her behaviour at times. Almost immediately she hit the streets, senior officers requested that she be sent back to college for further training. She was frequently put through supervisory review, and by August of her first year on the job serious doubts about her suitability were being expressed.

But, New Orleans needed police officers; the city was not prepared to pay its law enforcers a proper wage, and the politicians were desperate to be seen to be addressing the racial problems that many felt would blow up into full scale riot at some point. Politicians and senior officers certainly played their part in creating the circumstances through which the soon to unfold tragedy would come about. It was their policies that allowed an unsuitable candidate to become a qualified police officer.

Further, in real life little is ever properly black and white. And despite her dubious early performance in some areas, she did have some success. She was, ironically in the light of what would follow, extremely community conscious and won the Officer of the Month award for her work in this field.

There was a certain Bonnie and Clyde element to Antoinette Frank's crimes. Not in the romantic, almost heroic way in which these two are treated today, especially in Hollywood and aspects of the media. But love – maybe infatuation – appears to have played a part in her actions.

Eighteen months into her work Antoinette was called to an incident that would change her life. On November 25th 1994, she was the officer called to attend a shooting crime. The victim was one Rogers Lacaze. He was hardly a person deserving of much in the way of sympathy. A known drug dealer, he was a member of the criminal fraternity.

Some confusion exists over the beginning of the relationship between Antoinette and Lacaze. Investigators would later identify this event as the first meeting point between the two, although Frank herself insists that they had in fact met several months before.

Whichever of these is the case, what is not in question is that the relationship between the two grew quickly as Lacaze recovered from the shooting. Antoinette was a strikingly attractive woman, but she was drawn to the roguish persona of Lacaze. A professional relationship between police officer and victim of crime (if victim is the right word to apply to a criminal such as Lacaze) quickly blossomed into a friendship. In turn, this friendship soon ignited into a full on sexual relationship.

Antoinette displayed extremely poor judgement in the case. She faced losing her career through just having such a relationship with a man very much on the police department's radar. What she then allowed her boyfriend to do put her in even greater jeopardy.

Whether any attempt was made to keep the relationship secret is not known; if there was such an effort, it was remarkably naïve and unsuccessful. Firstly, the well known to police drug dealer was spotted driving his new girlfriend's car. Concerns soon escalated when he was even observed moving her police unit after she was deployed at the scene of an accident.

Another time, Lacaze accompanied her on a police call. She was attending a complaint and took her boyfriend along for the ride, introducing him to the member of the public as a 'trainee officer'. At other times, she claimed the younger man was her nephew.

Soon, what might, with a generous spirit, be interpreted as innocent and ill thought through japes turned into more serious matters. Testimony against her said that she and Lacaze would pull over cars, as though on police business, then proceed to rob them.

These crimes were the forerunners to even more serious misdemeanours. Soon, with Lacaze in tow, minor robberies from cars would turn into a major attempt to steal from a secondary work place, and that, in turn, would lead to murder.

Later, still pleading innocence of any wrong doing, Frank largely refused to discuss her relationship with Lacaze with investigating officers, other than to say that she was trying to help the former shooting victim. Faced with virtually any question, her response to investigators was limited to 'look it up in the record.' As it came out, slowly, that she and Lacaze had engaged in a sexual relationship, she tried to defend this by saying that she would not judge the man on the basis of his past crimes.

Yet she was on shaky ground. The day prior to her murders she was observed trying to buy 9mm ammunition from a Walmart store. Her defence for this was that, as a police officer, she was entitled to purchase arms.

But in the month before this, there was evidence that her relationship with Lacaze, particularly with regards to their nefarious activities, were escalating. John Stevens and Anthony Wallace claimed in court, at Lacaze's trial, that they had met Lacaze at a party in early February 1995. As the two men were leaving the party, an argument blew up between Lacaze and Stevens. Wallace said that they should leave, but the two men were stopped by police after a few blocks.

It was no surprise that the driver of the police vehicle was Antoinette Frank. She ordered the two men out of their car, and next they saw Lacaze exit the police car armed with a pistol. A fight ensued involving all four, and when another man tried to intervene, Frank shouted that Lacaze was 'the good guy.'

Back up arrived in the form of civil sheriff Irvin Bryant. He saw Wallace run from the fight and pick up a gun, which he ordered him to drop. Wallace did so immediately, but was arrested and charged with attempted murder and armed robbery. Police did not call, at any point, for Bryant's testimony in this matter.

In order to supplement her meagre police salary, Antoinette worked on an occasional, part time basis as a security guard at a Vietnamese restaurant, called the Kim Anh. This was located in New Orleans East and was a local business run by the Vu family. It was in the early hours of March 4th 1995 that Antoinette and Lacaze visited Kim Anh at the restaurant. They had already visited a couple of times earlier that night to pick up left overs from the meals the family served. By now the restaurant was closed. Some of the family were conducting the nightly clean while Chau Vu disappeared into the kitchen to check the night's takings.

Although Frank was not working that night as the off duty security guard she sometimes became, another police officer was. It cannot be emphasised enough that back in the 1990s, pay was extremely poor for those (mostly) civically minded citizens who risked their lives keeping the streets of New Orleans as safe as they could. When not uniformed up and patrolling the highways and alleyways of the impoverished city, many of the department's employees undertook additional opportunities to earn enough money to feed and home themselves and their families.

Indeed, many commentators blame the poor working conditions, especially regarding pay, as a driving force behind the fact that so many New Orleans officers of the time became embroiled in corrupt activities.

However, this does not seem to be an excuse that can be used by Antoinette Frank.

Chau Vu took some of the night's takings to slip to the off duty policemen who had been working as a security officer there that night, Ronald A Williams II. This young man, in his mid-twenties, was a father of two. He had been an officer for under three years. His youngest son was just one week old. The boy would grow up with no memories of a father he had barely met.

Following one of the earlier visits of Frank that evening, Chau had noticed that she could not find her door key after the officer left. This time, it soon became clear that Lacaze and Frank were approaching the restaurant with the intention of taking more than a few mouthfuls of left over treats.

Antoinette Frank used the key she had stolen to open the locked front door. She passed Williams quickly, and pushed Chau, along with her brother Quoc and another employee of the restaurant towards the kitchen.

Unsure what was happening, Williams made to follow, but was stopped in his tracks by the sound of gunshots. The next thing he knew, he was on the floor. The shots had been fired by Lacaze who, slipping behind the off duty officer, had shot him in the neck, severing his spinal cord and paralysing him in a moment.

Lacaze was not finished. As Williams lay prostrate and helpless, the drug dealer continued to shoot him; firstly in the head and then in the back. The wounds he endured proved fatal. Distracted by the shots, which suggests that this course of action was not in their plans, Frank turned back towards the dining room. Chau and Quoc desperately sought somewhere to hide. Having seen their security guard murdered, who can guess at the fear they must have experienced in that moment?

The brother and sister led their terrified employee into the large walk in cooler located in the kitchen. They turned out the light and prayed. Not just for themselves, but also for Ha and Cuong, their other brother and sister who were still out in the restaurant, in serious danger.

Peering through a tiny gap in the cooler door, the restaurant owners could make out a part of the kitchen. They saw Frank desperately hunting for something – it soon became apparent that it was the night's takings. Other shots were fired and Frank roared out for the location of the money.

The next thing the brother and sister saw was that upholder of law and order, Antoinette Frank, hitting their brother Cuong with her pistol demanding to know where the money was to be found. Finally, after hesitation, he indicated the microwave, and the robber took the cash from its hiding place. But she was not finished. As twenty one year old Ha was pleading for her life, Frank shot her three times in a frenzy of bloodshed. Next, she poured six more bullets into Cuong. He was just seventeen years of age.

Frank and Lacaze began to make their way from the restaurant. Meanwhile, Quoc fled to a friend who lived nearby to call 911, while

Chau tried to call the police on her cell phone. But the cooler prevented any signal from being gained.

Meanwhile, Antoinette had dropped Lacaze off at a nearby apartment. Both were aware that there were witnesses at the restaurant, although they were unsure exactly what they might have seen. Antoinette heard her police radio report that there was an officer down at the Kim Anh Restaurant. She grabbed a patrol car and made the instant decision to head there, adopting the role of an attending officer. She thought that if she could be the first to arrive, she might have the opportunity to silence Chau and Quoc.

She entered the restaurant through the back door, identifying herself as a police officer, but Chau said: 'I know what you've done!' and fled to the front dining room, just as other officers arrived. Chau blurted out what had happened, and the chance for Frank to kill the witnesses to her crime was gone.

Despite that, Frank continued to deny any involvement in the night's fatal activities.

'She's the most cold hearted person I've ever encountered in three decades as an officer,' said Eddie Rantz, the detective who was assigned the case.

Police questioned both Frank and Chau there and then, with the two seated at different tables in the restaurant. Antoinette was charged with three counts of first degree murder on the spot, and escorted to the station. Lacaze was arrested a couple of hours later.

While under questioning, Frank eventually buckled and confessed to the crimes. She said that robbery had not been their main intention. She and Lacaze had gone to the restaurant because they thought that Williams, the other police officer who worked as a part time security guard, had been taking more than his fair share of work and pay on offer at the Kim Anh. They had just wished to redress the balance. For her deeds, Antoinette Frank became the first New Orleans police officer to be charged with killing a fellow lawman.

She and Lacaze were indicted by grand jury in April of 1995. Lacaze went to trial first, was found guilty and sentenced to death. The crucial evidence that secured his conviction was that he had used his victim's, Ronald Williams', credit card within minutes of the killing and robbery. It was enough to persuade the jury of his guilt.

Two months later, on September 5th 1995, it was Antoinette Frank's turn to face the consequences of her actions in a court room. It was not a long process. The defence called precisely none of the forty witnesses they had in hand, apparently falsely hoping that the prosecution would fail to prove their case. They were wrong, and the jury took just twenty two minutes to convict the former police officer on all counts. Back then, it was the shortest time a jury had been out before returning a guilty verdict in a New Orleans murder trial.

The next day, they took only twice that time to decide that Antoinette should face the death penalty for her crimes. Sentencing took place on October 20th 1995, and she was incarcerated on Death Row at the Louisiana Correctional Institute for Women.

And that should have been that. Crimes had been committed, particularly savage and cruel ones. Eye witnesses had observed the offences. A jury had convicted both perpetrators with little, if any, doubt. Both should, by today, have been executed, twenty three years after their convictions. But in capital murder cases events have a way of twisting and turning in unexpected directions as attorneys seek to save the lives of their clients.

The first unusual factor to surface related to Antoinette's abusive father. The strength of blood relationships can overcome many atrocities, and despite the harm that the young policewoman had suffered at his hands as a child, in 1993 she had accepted him into her home.

But shortly into his stay, he disappeared and in the end Antoinette officially reported him as missing. No progress was made until, in November of 1995 (the month following Frank's receipt of the death sentence) police discovered a human skull buried under her house. A bullet hole gave clear indication as to the cause of the owner's death.

It is the belief of both police and prosecutors that those remains are of Antoinette's father, Adam. They are also convinced that he was another victim of the young woman, albeit one for whom far less sympathy can be held.

But with Antoinette already facing a death sentence, police have not sought to find out more. Writer Chuck Hustmyre holds a special interest in the killings committed by Antoinette Frank, and has written a book on the subject. In 2005, he concluded: 'As for those human bones unearthed beneath Frank's house, so far authorities have made no serious effort to identify them. The (back then) 10 year old case, they say, remains under investigation.'

Then, in 2006, Frank's legal team sought to overturn her death penalty. If a killer is to lose their life, it is essential that every aspect of their trial is studied to best ensure that no errors have been made. Unfortunately, American legal history is littered with accounts of (mostly) men sent to their deaths when, later, evidence emerges that casts doubt on their guilt.

In this case, the attorneys were not disputing that their client had committed the crimes. However, the growing understanding of people's mental state that had emerged following recent foreign conflicts in which the United States had been involved suggested some mitigating circumstances might exist.

Her legal team knew from evidence that Antoinette had suffered a very unpleasant childhood. Developing understanding of post traumatic stress disorder showed that people exposed to such incidents could, later in life, act in ways against which their early experiences mitigated. Frank, claimed the lawyers, had not been given enough state funded support to raise post traumatic stress disorder as a possible mitigation at the sentencing stage of her trial. Because of this, they argued, the death penalty she was facing should be overturned, and commuted to one of life imprisonment.

However, proving such matters is notoriously difficult. In part that is because so little is still understood (even less more than a decade ago) about psychological effects on the human brain. Further, a cynicism exists towards defences offered by the legal teams of convicted killers. If their client is facing death, goes the argument, they will do what they can to prevent this. Finally, the adversarial system of justice favoured in American courts means that people take sides. Judges then have to follow one side or the other. A state psychiatrist was happy to identify Antoinette Frank's mental condition as being one suffering from a narcissistic personality disorder, and that was not enough to mitigate against her crimes.

The Supreme Court in Louisiana was happy with this diagnosis, and the death penalty was upheld. Following this decision District Judge Frank Marullo decided, in April 2008, to sign Antoinette's death warrant. She was scheduled to die by lethal injection in under three months. However, the Louisiana Supreme Court issued a stay of execution for 90 days, but with suspiciously speedy timing, the moment that stay ended the same judge signed a new death warrant

This time, Antoinette's execution was calendared for December 8th of that year.

This was too little time for defence attorneys to review the huge records of testimony and evidence they faced before the deadline for appeals hit. So, in late November, two weeks before the former police office was due to be latched to the gurney, the Supreme Court decided to overturn Judge Marullo's decision. Her new attorney of the time, Gary Clements, was clear that this was the right decision. 'She has a lot of litigation to go,' he said. 'I am quite confident that Judge Marullo knows this and is fully aware (that a stay will be granted).'

Having signed two death warrants already, the second with undue haste, the defence team sought to have Marullo recused from the case.

Although this did not initially succeed, a strange turn then emerged. It was Marullo's own signature that appeared on an order which allowed Frank to take the gun used in the murders from the evidence room. Although the judge always maintained that the signature was forged, enough of a doubt was raised in the shady backwater that is, occasionally, Louisiana law for the judge to be forced to step down from the case.

It was not just Antoinette whose case was undergoing a tide of changes. Her partner in crime, Rogers Lacaze saw his conviction overturned and a new trial ordered in 2015. It turned out that a juror in the case had failed to declare that he was a state trooper and had been a railroad law enforcement officer.

At the time of the trial, people with such careers were barred from sitting on a jury in a murder trial. But the decision to overturn Lacaze's conviction was itself overturned later, when an appellate court decided that the evidence against the killer was too strong to justify a new trial. Many felt that decision was strange in a death sentence case, where no stone should be left unturned in the search for absolute truth.

And what of the surviving members of the Vu family, the primary victims in this case? After the tragedy that had befallen their family, they tried to keep their restaurant business going, and indeed succeeded for another ten years. Then, in 2005, another terrible event was to strike. The restaurant was severely damaged in the floods that submerged New Orleans in the wake of Hurricane Katrina. If that was not enough, the looting that followed this natural disaster saw the Vu's home targeted.

Among the objects taken in the storm's aftermath was the jewellery Ha and Cuong had been wearing the night they were killed. It was the final straw for the Vietnamese family. They sold their location and upped sticks to a better area of the city, where they felt safer from both human and natural interventions.

And so Antoinette Frank and Rogers Lacaze remain waiting for the day that their cases reach the top of the docket list. The day that a date for their execution is set and this time, the appeals run out. The day they are led to the table and strapped down, before life ending chemicals are allowed to flow into their bodies.

This is the consequence they face for a flurry of Bonnie and Clyde type robberies that got out of control, and ended in murder. It is just that, on this occasion, Bonnie was not a waitress living her mother, but a fully fledged police officer. The public expects more from such people.

SERIAL KILLING COP : THE TRUE STORY OF MIKHAIL POPKOV

16

FRANK COLEMAN

'He is charming and sociable. Women like him but he is a beast inside, and it is always hard to fight a werewolf.' - Mikhail Zavorin, police investigator

Mikhail Popkov may be the most prolific serial killers in world history.

He led a double-life as a family man with a wife and a young daughter. But after the dissolution of the Soviet Union, Popkov was able to take advantage of the lack of police authority to get away with his most barbaric fantasies.

Using his police uniform as a cover, he would lure unsuspecting women into his squad car where he would drive them to an isolated forest to kill them. His murders would go unabated for close to twenty years until Russian authorities finally utilized DNA evidence to match Popkov with the killings.

He was able to evade authorities because he was the authority.

Both he and his wife were police officers.

This is their story.

THE ORIGINS OF A KILLER

Mikhail Popkov was born on March 7th, 1964 in Russia. Little is known about his early life. He was a sporting youth like any other before entering the police academy. He would meet and marry Elene who was a fellow officer. The two would have a daughter, Ekaterina, who would later become a schoolteacher.

"I had a family," Popkov said. "My wife and daughter considered me a good husband and father, which corresponded to reality. I was in the service, in the police, having positive feedback on my work. I never thought of myself as mentally unhealthy. During my police service, I regularly passed medical commissions and was recognized as fit."

Accounts vary over what set off Popkov. His first known killing occurred in 1992 when he was twenty-eight years old. Most serial killers start showing anti-social behavior early in childhood. But Popkov is an anomaly in that there doesn't appear to be any early warning signs.

Popkov would claim that he never intended to become a serial killer and that it "just happened."

"I just felt I wanted to kill a woman I was give a lift to in my car," he said of his first victim in 1992.

The belief that his wife was having an affair with one of his co-workers, did seem to set him off course. His wife denied this claim vehemently but Popkov discovered two used condoms thrown in the garbage at his home. His wife claims that the condoms were used by some friends who were visiting for the night.

"I just had some reasons to suspect her," Popkov said. "I'm not looking for excuses, but this was the impetus for my future."

Fueled by a jealous rage, he began seeking out women that reminded him of his wife's sluttish ways.

Another theory is that he targeted women who reminded him of his mother. This is a typical Freudian response when assessing the motivation of serial killers who murder women...They are symbolically killing their mother.

In Popkov's case, however, this doesn't seem to hold weight. His mother would go on to the defend her son even when the evidence against him proved to be overwhelming. By all accounts, she seemed to have been a loving and doting mother to her "Mischa" as she called him.

THE ROUTINE

Popkov had an established modus operandi for abducting his victims. His targets would be women alone, often those who were drunk.

He would put on his police uniform and park his car outside discos and restaurants, waiting for a tipsy woman to come wobbling out. He would then lure her into his car with the promise of a ride.

"I could arrest you," Popkov would sometimes tell his victims. "But I'm feeling charitable. Get in and I'll take you home."

Other times, he would play the role of a cop looking out for a young woman's best interest.

"There have been reports of a man attacking women around here," he would tell the victim in a conspiratorial tone. "Let me take you home. We can't have you walking out on the streets alone."

Once inside his vehicle, however, Popkov would drive his trusting victim to an isolated forest. Once there he would force them to strip naked for him. He would become enraged, attacking them with whatever weapon he had on hand. Sometimes he used an axe, sometimes he used a knife while others he strangled to death. He would decapitate one of the victims and ripped out the heart of another.

"The choice of weapons for killing was always casual," Popkov said. "I never prepared beforehand to commit a murder. I would use any object that was in the car - a knife, an axe, a bat."

Then he would rape the victim post-mortem.

He would not go to great lengths to dump the body to avoid discovery. The attack would take place in an isolated area and he would leave bodies in the forest the side of the road and sometimes the cemetery.

Popkov nicknamed himself "The Cleaner", stating that it became his "misson" to rid the Russian streets of loose women.

"I had a double life," Popkov said. "In one life I was an ordinary person ... In my other life I committed murders, which I carefully concealed from everyone, realizing that this was a criminal offense."

"The victims were those who, unaccompanied by men, at night, without a certain purpose, were on the streets, behaving carelessly, who were not afraid to enter into conversation with me, get into my car, and then go for a drive in search of adventures, for the sake of entertainment, ready to drink alcohol and have sexual intercourse with me. Not all women became victims, but those of a certain negative behavior, I had a desire to teach and punish."

THE SOLE SURVIVOR

In 1998, he would attack a woman later referred to in the press as "Svetlana M."

Svetlana was fifteen but according to police looked older than her actual age.

She told investigators that a police car pulled up next to her and offered her a ride. Unsuspecting, she got into the vehicle where she was driven to a nearby forest.

Following his standard routine, Popkov ordered the girl to take off all her clothes. He then smashed her head against a tree and knocked her out.

He would violate her then leave her for dead.

The next day, Svetlana would be found, somehow still alive despite being completely naked in the sub-zero temperatures of the region.

She would awaken in the hospital and tell the police her story.

"She was unconscious because of severe head injuries," Nikolai Kitaev, one of the police investigators said. "Police did not start a criminal investigation for a long time despite numerous complaints from the girl's mother. Finally, Svetlana would be questioned and told in detail about her rapist-policeman and his car."

Police didn't believe her story. Svetlana, however, would identify Popkov as her attacker after she was shown a photograph of him in a police car. Police would question Popkov, who laughed it off. They also questioned his wife who stated that he was with her the whole night.

With an alibi by a trusted police officer let alone his wife, the police didn't pursue the matter any further.

"She (Svetlana) clearly confirmed it was him," Kitaev said. "But again, the police trusted Mikhail's wife - once more she composed an alibi for him and the criminal investigation was stopped and sent to the archives."

"It was enough just to perform a DNA test of this man but the police interrogated Popkov's wife who composed an alibi for her husband. Later he became more careful and carried on with his horrific crimes."

Knowing they had a serial killer/rapist on their hands, Russian investigators worked to construct a psychological profile of who their suspect could be. They surmised that he may be either a metalworker, bus/driver, railroad worker or heating station engineer. They were also convinced that he may also have been a mortuary worker because so many bodies had been found at or near cemeteries.

Still, Popkov didn't have to do much to evade authorities. Russian investigators were still disorganized after the fall of the Soviet Union. He was able to elude and evade detection by simply being a little more organized than the people investigating him. It didn't take much, he knew their strengths and weaknesses...after all, he was one of them.

"There are two groups of maniacs - organized and non-organized," Russian psychiatrist Alexander Grishin said. "Non-organized maniacs are easy to catch, their crimes are quickly solved - they are people with psychiatric pathologies, who live in their own world, they are hiding from people, often untidy. Organized maniacs - Popkov is a good example - are people with high mental abilities, socially adapted, often with families, they find convenient jobs which secures them and gives time for crimes. It is a hard job to catch such a maniac, it is hard to spot such a person, even police enrollment tests are not good enough for it. The fact that only drunk women attracted him could be the result of his childhood problems and associations - his mother used to drink alcohol and often abused him. Maybe in his childhood other drunk women abused him too, and all this affected his behavior later in his adult life and led to such horrible consequences."

INCOMPETENCE LEADS TO MORE KILLINGS

The failure of the police authority to suspect Popkov coupled with his wife covering for him allowed him to murder several more women over the ensuing years.

One of those victims was Tanya Chagaeva, a 29-year old housewife with a daughter at home.

Tanya had received an invitation to go to a concert. Despite protestations from her husband who wanted her to stay home, Tanya wanted to take in the experience.

"It happened 15 year ago but the pain does not go away - it was me who presented Tanya a ticket to go to a concert, and she was killed after attending it', Viktoria Chagaeva, Tanya's sister said.

Her husband Igor was against his wife going to the concert but she would go anyway with her girlfriend, Yulia. The two would leave their home but not return.

Igor would call Viktoria in the morning, asking if his wife had gone to stay with her sister. They both then realized that Tanya was missing.

"I got truly scared," Viktoria said. "It was the first time, she had never done this before. There were no mobile phones at that time, we could only call Yulia's parents thinking Tanya must have stayed overnight there for some reason. But Yulia's parents said she had not come home either."

The police would prove to be of little help. They told the families that they would have to wait three days before the women could be qualified as a missing person.

Later that night, a farmer would find the naked bodies of both women in a village close to Angarsk.

"It was 1am when Tanya's husband Igor and I came to the police," Viktoria recalled. "We did not tell our mother yet. Igor was absolutely devastated and only repeated - 'She was killed, she was killed'. I was shocked too, but I simply could not believe it and replied - 'what are you talking about?' Later we were told that their bodies were found next to each other, both girls were raped, cut and chopped. The experts told us that at first they were killed then raped. My elder brother Oleg went to the morgue to identify Tanya. He had flown from Moscow immediately. He felt sick when saw the body, she was so mutilated. He was almost green when he came out of there - he just could not say a word. I did not dare to go in and look."

The police had already established the chain of events. Both Tanya and Yulia had left the concert and went out for a drink with some friends. Leaving the bar, they were then offered a ride by a policeman.

"Only the fact that this bastard was in a police uniform explains why Tanya got into his car," Viktoria said. "Many people attended Tanya's funeral. It felt as if the whole town was there. Our poor mother lost her consciousness several times, she needed a lot of medicine to cope. Igor was in almost the same condition. Tanya's coffin was open, her face was not hurt. He damaged the back of her skull, and her body was heavily cut. Yulia's coffin was closed, her face was cut up and disfigured."

Tanya's mother would never be the same.

"She felt as if she had died with Tanya, life became useless for her. She lived only because she was visiting various mediums one by one, looking for the killer and wasting her money. Nobody gave her any serious information but she kept doing it. She died in 2007 aged 66 from a heart attack. I think her heart could not cope with the pain any longer."

A REIGN OF TERROR

In August of 1999, Popkov would offer a medical student a ride. He would take her to the forest and chop off her head, stabbing her six times before stuffing down a garbage chute. Later that month he approached twenty-year old Maria Molotkova. Maria was leaving work from a water pumping station when Popkov offered her a ride. Maria was unsuspecting of the police officer, just like all the rest. He would drive her to the forest, kill then violate her corpse.

In June of 2000, he would claim two of his older victims, 35-year old Marina Lyzhina and 37-year old Lilia Pashkovskaya.

Marina and Lilia worked at the same shop and left to see Marina's sister. They worked late and started to walk home around midnight. They were going to call a taxi cab but changed their minds. The night was warm and they decided to walk.

Until Popkov came along in his police vehicle and picked the women up.

Popkov would murder the women but realize that he left his police badge behind at the scene.

"I found the token (badge) right away, but saw that one of the women was still breathing," Popkov said. "I was shocked by the fact that she was still alive. I finished her with a shovel."

The two women were buried in closed coffins. Their bodies had been so mutilated that the Russian tradition of having open coffins had to be disregarded. Marina had a 14-year old daughter. Lilia had two children, a 12-year old daughter and 3-year old son.

He then targeted a music teacher at his daughter's school.

"Her corpse was found in the forest along with the body of another woman," Popkov said. "My daughter asked me to give her money, because the school was collecting to organize funerals. I gave [it to] her."

Popkov then step down from his policemen duties. He would find work in the security business, working as a guard for the Angarsk Oil and Chemical company.

FALSE CLAIMS?

Popkov would claim that he stopped killing when he became impotent as he contracted syphilis from one of his victims. There is no word if he transferred the disease to his wife as well.

The press would dub him as "The Wednesday Murder" as that was the day his victims were typically found. One detective working on the case would refer to him as a "werewolf."

It is reported that he did not stop killing after he contracted the sexually transmitted disease. Investigators are still looking at murders from the time he worked as a traveling security guard.

ARREST

On June 23rd, 2012, Popkov would be arrested in Vladivostok when he was buying a car. He had his DNA sampled along with 3,500 other police officers and his sample was matched with the semen he left behind on his victims.

"I could not anticipate the examination of DNA," Popkov said to investigators. "I was born in another century. Now there are such modern technologies, methods, but not earlier. If we have not got to that level of genetic examination, then ... I would not be sitting in front of you."

After Popkov's identity was revealed to the press, Tanya Chagaeva's sister Viktoria realized that she knew the man.

They had both competed in a biathlon at the same gym.

"I was stuck with horror when I saw the picture of this maniac in the paper and online," Viktoria said. "My sister's killer was looking into my eyes. I immediately felt as if I'd met him. Looking at him, I could hardly breathe. Some minutes later I looked at him another time and thought - oh my God, I know him! I was so shocked, I even took a knife and cut his face in the newspaper, I needed to let this horror out of me. I remember him as a tall slim man, he was always alone, with a slippery and shifty glance. I think such people just must not live. This beast took the life of my sister, who had so many happy years in front of her. I cried a lot that day, but it is time to be quiet and just wait. He will be punished by law and criminals in jail will punish him too, I am sure he will pay for all the murders one day...."

His fellow police officers who worked with him were shocked as well.

"When I read about him in the press I literally choked," said Dmitry Valuev. "Because I used to work with him and thought I knew him. He was an absolutely normal man. He liked biathlon; once on duty he shot a rapist during an arrest. There was an investigation and he was not punished, the chiefs considered he had taken fair action."

"I used to work closely with him for 5 years," Sergey Golovkin said. "He knew lots of jokes and stories, and could be soul of the party."

His own daughter was shocked. To this day, she does not believe that her father committed those murders

"I do not believe any of this," Ekaterina said. "I always felt myself as 'Daddy's girl'. For 25 years we were together, hand in hand. We walked, rode bikes, went to the shops, and he met me from school. We both collect model cars, so we have the same hobby.

"I wanted to be a criminologist, so I read a book with tips of how investigators catch serial killers and there were also basic classifications [about murderers]. Daddy doesn't fit any of these classifications - he doesn't look like some maniac."

But Ekaterina recently changed her tone, not having seen her father for over two years. She expressed a desire to "look into his eyes and understand if he really could be that killer"

Popkov's wife continues to support him although she no longer offers alibis. She would describe the charges against the husband as "fairy tales".

"We met on the Monday and Tuesday before sentencing and discussed this situation," Elena Popkov said. "He already knew that it would be a life sentence. He denied everything. Even when our daughter Katya asked him, he said, 'Katya, you understand that all these [allegations] are fairy tales. It is the system - I have worked within it, I know this system well. We have been married for 28 years. If I suspected something wrong, of course, I would divorce with him. I support him, I believe him. If he were to be released right now, I would not say a word and we would continue to live together. I love him, I support him. He did not cause me any harm for all these years. I felt safe with him."

Elena would not be the only woman to step up and defend Popkov. His mother would address the press as well and express her support.

"I cannot believe he walked alone to the forest in a police uniform," Popkov's mother said. "Where was the blood? His clothes should have been covered in blood or if he had tried to wash the blood away, the clothes would have been wet. His wife would definitely have noticed all that. He loves his family, cherishes his daughter, and he dreamed about grandchildren. He would not have done this. He will remain my son, until my death. He studied well and from the very beginning he was excellent pupil. He loved to cook, pancakes or something like this and he was very neat, like me."

But even his own mother had her doubts...

"Misha (Mikhail), give us some sign if you have done all this or not. And if so, why? It is hard to live knowing nothing. We need to know."

Popkov was initially suspected of killing twenty-nine women. Twenty-five of the women were aged 19 to 28 while four were between the ages of 35 to 40. All victims lived in Angarsk, Irkutsk.

Later, however, the Russian authorities admitted that the numbers were considerably higher after they interrogated Popkov.

"To clarify the numbers, Popkov has confessed to 59 new murders," Irkutsk Investigative Committee spokeswoman Karina Golovacheva said. "We are not counting in this total those 22 for which he was already sentenced. These cases are already closed. So there are 59 new murders. That means, if we add them to the earlier 22, it will be 81 murders in total."

Popkov would charged with an additional forty-seven murders with another twelve still pending.

"We are quite sure about the 12 other cases," Golovacheva said. "We are now gathering all the evidence. Further analysis of the evidence is underway and 'in the nearest future we can bring charges in these 12 cases' which Popkov has already admitted"

Based on Popkov's confession it appears that he is the most prolific serial killer in Russia history. He has a higher kill count that Andrei Chikatilo, aka the Butcher of Rostov, who had been convicted of over fifty-three murders. Alexander Pichushkin and Anatoly Onoprienko were convicted of fifty-two and forty-nine respectively.

But authorities now believe that he is "rationing out his confessions" as he is delaying his time in the Russian jail system before being sentenced to serve out the rest of his life in a brutal penal colony where he will be forced into hard labor.

Because he traveled so much after leaving his police job, authorities believe that Popkov is responsible for even more murders than already suspected.

Alexander Pichushkin - the Bitsa Park Maniac

*Stranger than **Fiction***

In 2010, journalist Denis Faye sat down with industry expert Pat Brown in an attempt to bridge the gap between how serial killers are portrayed in film and television and how they are in real life. Brown quickly cuts through the existing information floating around on this disparity.

> *"Faye: So what does Hollywood get right about serial killers?*
> *Brown: Very little."*

In the case of "real life" serial killer Alexander Pichushkin, known as the infamous Bitsa Maniac, the Chessboard Killer, and arguably one of Russia's most consummate serial killer, it's almost impossible to draw the line between fact and fiction. Between his mysterious past, the inventiveness of the press, and his own fabrications, Pichushkin's story requires an eye for the difference between killers from the silver screen and true monsters.

Described as a "real-life criminal profiler," Pat Brown has a lot to say about the difference between the fictional serial killers we see in movies and television and the all too real murderers we catch glimpses of in the news. In an interview with the WGA, she attempted to outline some of the most prominent errors writers make when depicting serial killers. She immediately honed in on the false complexity that writers default to in order to create drama, lamenting that such specificity is almost never the case.

> *"They're not as bizarre as the films show... [They] tend to over-profile the killer's mental state."*

In the news, Alexander Pichushkin's story has been sensationalized and stretched, the gaps in his narrative filled with fiction. Between 1992 and 2006 Pichushkin was responsible for the deaths of up to 62 people, putting him in the running for being one of Russia's most prolific serial killers. But despite this infamy and attention, there are plenty of holes in the account of his killing spree for reporters to expound and invent. Even Pichushkin's Wikipedia entry contains an entirely fictional tale of his childhood inspired solely by his title as the Chessboard Killer. This moniker may be the most popular and certainly most evocative option for Pichushkin, but it is by no means the most accurate. Those who were most affected by this slew of murders and know the most about them, locals and experts alike, all prefer the more succinct and accurate name Pichushkin had earned: the Maniac.

Creating a *Monster*

Psychologists often argue whether the monstrousness of serial killers is born or made by trauma or environment. On one hand, being able to point a finger at exactly what caused a human being to do such horrible things can be comforting, but all too often external factors are used to distance killers from blame and evoke sympathy. Brown laments that this distancing is what she is most opposed to in the portrayal of serial killers. "I've never seen a serial killer with redeeming qualities or one you can have some kind of sympathy for, like it's just a bad hobby he's got." On the other hand, a world with the potential for people who are simply born to commit heinous murders is a scary one to imagine, and given the number of environmental similarities between serial killers, one that frankly doesn't seem to exist.

Currently, the prevailing argument is that it is a combination of the natural and nurtured elements of someone's personality that react upon one another to create a psychopath, though Brown feels there is more of a conscious choice involved. "He's just pissed off at society and became a psychopath when life didn't work out his way..." In the case of Pichushkin, close analysis of his childhood, family, and early social interactions reveal many of the trademarks common in other serial killers, however, Brown's reminder of free will is an important one to keep in mind. While Pichushkin's childhood has some traumatic roots, ultimately he was not *made* into a monster—he *chose* to commit murder, and on a minimum of 52 separate occasions.

On April 9th, 1974 Alexander Pichushkin was born in Mytishchi, Moscow, and according to his mother, Natasha Pichushkina, he was a normal child as far as she could tell. Alexander, or Sasha for short, lived in a modest one bedroom apartment with his father and mother who had grown up in that same apartment. The complex is one of many on the outskirts of Moscow, a decaying remainder of soviet era infrastructure and some of the only reasonably priced housing in the area. Nicknamed *khrushchevki* after Nikita Khrushchev, the spartan public housing lacks charm and personality, but continues to serve in functionality and affordability. A mere nine months after Sasha is born, his father leaves Natasha to raise their son alone.

"I tried to raise him like a normal mother... I know now that I raised my son very poorly... [but] I can't say what I did wrong."

Besides his mother's account in a popular interview from 2007, not much is known about young Sasha's childhood. One of the few verified details of Sasha's childhood is the head trauma he incurred at the age of four when he fell backward off a swing outside the *khrushchevki* only for it to swing toward him again and strike his forehead. Immediately following the incident he spent time in an institution for the disabled, though exactly how long he stayed there is not reported. Brain injuries, specifically to the frontal lobe where Sasha was struck, are very common among serial killers. David Berkowitz, Leonard Lake,

Kenneth Bianchi, and John Gacy all suffered similar head trauma early in life, which neuroscientists link to violence and impulse control issues, as well as emotional and empathetic difficulties.

There are plenty of other mixed and unsubstantiated accounts of torment in Sasha's childhood inflicted by bullies instead of by accident, including one anecdote about a group of children ganging up on Sasha to steal his moped. A police investigator offered a possible explanation in an interview, saying that "Pichushkin" is a name with an effeminate, weak connotation, a detail that would otherwise be lost to the cultural barrier. Entrenched in a Russian cultural context often tinged with homophobia and toxic ideas of masculinity, young Sasha had his cards stacked against him. With the effeminate name, an absent father, a stint in an institution, and very few, if any, friends, he was ideal fodder for grade school bullies. Despite Pichushkin eventually outgrowing his childhood weaknesses and becoming a model image of Russian masculinity, many experts speculate that he might not be heterosexual.

Mentioned only briefly in an interview with the lead investigator, the question of the Bitsa Maniac's sexuality was quickly brushed off. Pichushkin smoked and drank, had a menial physical job stocking shelves at a grocery store, and a low voice with a gruff personality—to those surrounded by the cultural context of Russia's now-infamous homophobia, there was no possible way he could be anything but straight. Add in the brutal success of his murderous impulses and there is no hope of swaying the investigation's narrow image of Pichushkin.

His mother Natasha brought up in her 2007 interview that he never seemed to be interested in women or sex in general. His only documented emotional attachment is to a male classmate from his teens. An overwhelming majority of his victims, the people he was able to lure most easily and was most comfortable with, are all male ranging from as young as nine years old to retirement age. While there was never evidence of any sexual assault on his male victims to substantiate any of these claims, there also was a complete lack of sexual activity with his female victims as well. Based on the available, though sparse, information, it seems just as likely that Sasha lacked sexual impulse at all, and instead only had a lust to kill.

Yet another facet in the claims against Pichushkin's heterosexuality, young Sasha seemed to be heavily influenced by another serial killer, Andrei Chikatilo, whom he idolized to the extreme. Chikatilo's crimes came to light just as Sasha reached his most consciously formative years, and he kept careful track of his contemporary's every move. Chikatilo's spree of murders earned him the nickname of the Rostov Ripper, but he, like Sasha, was deemed by the press a maniac.

Finding **Inspiration**

In December of 1991 the newly liberated Russian media received news of an arrest made in relation to the series of unsolved, gruesome murders happening 117 miles northeast of Moscow, in Rostov von don. For nearly a decade the area had been terrorized by murders that were clearly linked to the same killer, who had been referred to as the Rostov Ripper. Immediately after the arrest, sensationalist news sources had yet to learn his name or see his photo, but had a brief summary of his crimes. His signature was stabbing, usually in excess of 30 times, gouging of the eyes, sexual assault, and evisceration; accused of 53 counts of murder in this style, the man whose name would later be learned became simply *the Maniac*. The public did not lay eyes upon the monster that they knew so little about until he appeared at the first day of his trial on April 14th the following year.

Just five days after Sasha's eighteenth birthday the media is suddenly saturated with the face of the Rostov Ripper, now revealed to be Andrei Chikatilo. His sallow face is pictured from behind iron bars throughout the trial, specially put in place of the usual plexiglass box, to protect him from the often hysterical and retaliatory relatives of his victims. These attacks were not the only noteworthy outbursts of the trial: Chikatilo and the judge, Leonid Akubzhanov, remained combative toward each other throughout the proceedings, with Chikatilo refusing to cooperate. Ignoring questions posed by the prosecution, Chikatilo's original well-spoken demeanor devolved into a show-stopping display of chaos, singing socialist anthems and exposing himself to the jury in an attempt to be deemed unfit to stand trial.

As the trial continued into the summer, news outlets revealed more of Chikatilo's gory past, full of sexual assault while in his teaching position, torturous excess during his killings, and the numerous occasions he was apprehended, questioned, or suspected before his final arrest. Sasha followed all of these stories with more than the morbid curiosity typical of a boy his age. He clipped articles from the papers and kept photos of Chikatilo's face, images with captions that described him as a "shaven-skulled demon" and articles detailing the horrific, decade long murder spree of *the Maniac*.

With the clarity of hindsight, Pichushkin's serial murders appear to be somewhat spawned from Chikatilo's, if not directly inspired. Teenaged Sasha was exposed to widespread press coverage of his killings and saw the attention he garnered from the public and his victims' families. He witnessed the controversy over Chikatilo's punishment, which arguably contributed to the suspension of Russia's death penalty in 1996 (notably, after executing yet another serial killer, Sergey Golovkin). At the very least, Pichushkin seemed intent on surpassing Chikatilo in number, keeping track of his alleged 61 victims with numbers pasted on his now-infamous chessboard. While journalists after the fact like to fixate on this chessboard and invent a final goal of filling it with 64 murders, Pichushkin never mentioned the board in his taped confession. Motivated only by his need to kill and desire to overshadow the Rostov Ripper, the lead police investigator doubted Pichushkin would stop when he ran out of squares.

"Pichushkin is quite an unusual serial killer he's a hunter, a typical hunter and his only motivation was to kill, there was no other motive, whatever else we might have thought."

*A New **Maniac** Begins*

On the 27th of July, Sasha takes his first step towards becoming the infamous Bitsa Maniac. Now three months after turning eighteen years old, he invites his friend and classmate Mikhail Odichuck to join him in something he has been ruminating possibly for years: to commit his first murder. For Pichushkin, this is the most intimate gesture he could possibly offer. Only a trusted friend, a confidante, someone he would deem worthy of sharing such a powerful experience of control and subversion of societal expectations could have been welcomed so wholly into Sasha's inner circle. Unfortunately for both boys, what Sasha viewed as a generous offer, Mikhail saw as a joke.

It would be easy to jump to the conclusion that Sasha held some form of fondness or affection towards his classmate Mikhail. With the seeming absence of his sexual attraction to women in combination with idolization of Chikatilo and experience being bullied as a child, their relationship could have even been interpreted as a boyhood crush. Out of 51 charges of murder and attempted murder, only three victims were female, a statistic that belies Pichushkin's gravitation toward men in general. At such an important developmental stage in his life, Sasha would be expected to display sexual and emotional attraction towards those he felt closest to at the time, namely his friend Mikhail. With over a decade of experience in examining the personalities of serial killers, specialist Pat Brown would insist otherwise.

"What people don't get is that a psychopath can portray, at certain points in his life, certain levels of affection... [but] those are just objects in his life... People are either useful, or they're in the way."

Mikhail made the mistake of getting in the way. Eventually the boy realized Sasha was dedicated to the idea of murder—and completely prepared. He knew to prey on the elderly and the homeless, strangers, who wouldn't be missed by family or valued by the police enough to warrant further investigation. He had already crafted the story of his "beloved" dog's grave in Bitsa Park as a trick to lure their victims with promise of a free drink, both lowering their victim's guard and impeding their ability to fight back. Most importantly, Sasha had discovered the manholes in Bitsa Park that fell up to 18 meters deep, full of highly pressurized currents, in which he would later dispose of twenty to thirty bodies. At exactly what point Mikhail came to the realization that Sasha was deadly serious, only Pichushkin knows—but his classmate never made it to the forest. That Monday afternoon Mikhail's lifeless body is found in the street, after dropping from a five-story balcony. Young Sasha was questioned by police, but they never suspected his involvement and ruled the tragedy a suicide with little to no other inquiry.

Prompted by Pichushkin's confession fifteen years later, a follow-up investigation examined Mikhail's body and discovered head trauma that didn't fit within expectations of impact on the ground. What they had glossed over appeared to be evidence that 18 year old Sasha had bashed in his classmate's head up to 21 times with an unidentifiable blunt object before lifting his lifeless body over the edge of the balcony to drop into the street below. Though the final result is similar to the neat, premeditated M.O. he would adopt later in life, this first murder was a crime of passion, fueled by betrayal and rage, and a moment Pichushkin would later look back on fondly.

"This first murder," he began in his televised confession, "It's like first love—It's unforgettable."

An Experimental Phase

For the next nine years, Pichushkin waits. Investigators speculated that Sasha repressed his homicidal urges for as long as possible, knowing that he would not be able to stop once he started again. Pichushkin neither confirmed nor denied these claims, and has offered no other explanation for such a long hiatus. But after those nine years are up, Sasha embarks on a personal journey with an astonishing body count, to discover all the ways he can kill and all the ways he can get away with it.

Now at the age of 27, Sasha began to mix up his M.O., experimenting with weapons, victims, and body disposal. The homeless were his first choice of victims, on whom he tested out another toss over the balcony and a homemade "pen shooter" Sasha had crafted himself; Pichushkin lamented in an interview that both of these methods were over too quickly. This second falling victim was only nine years old, whose death was overlooked just like Mikhail's. As for the pen shooter incident, Pichushkin later described the murder in his confession with explicit detail, from finding a homeless man sleeping on the street, to pressing the makeshift gun to his temple in broad daylight and watching him bleed. He explained that he had seen the man as an opportunity while he was walking to work and couldn't resist.

Eventually he moved on to victims who needed to be lured into the cover of the park, but these still would not be the bodies found by police and attributed to the Bitsa Maniac. The story Sasha told many of his victims centered on a "beloved" deceased dog, whose grave, he told them, was in the park. He would offer a drink of vodka over the nonexistent burial site to distract and relax them; little did they know that the spot he lead them to was strategically located by one of the manholes he had discovered in his youth. Sasha would then bash their heads on the manhole cover, only to open it and lift their inebriated or even unconscious bodies over the edge. His story varied slightly each time, and he continued to use opportunities like the sleeping homeless man to take advantage of poor drunks who wouldn't be missed amid his more focused strategy. Yet another distinction between fact and fiction, where news outlets attempted to fit all of Pichushkin's murders into a neat little box, Brown argues that just isn't so.

> *"[A real serial killer] doesn't have a fantastic signature with every crime, something really creepy that links every one of the crimes together … It's very exciting, but it's not the way it is in real life. He's not always going to use the same method. He might try something else on another day, so you have to be careful of that."*

When he later told police of his use of the sewer system to dispose of the corpses, they tested its validity by dropping a mannequin inside, only for it to be immediately torn apart by the forceful currents. They also later found the body of a missing person whose death Pichushkin had claimed fault of further into the system. Pichushkin blamed the police force's ineptitude for not being able to find the bodies he had so effectively destroyed. Normally the police would have to rely on what little evidence they have to corroborate a murderer's often fantastical claims and any particulars are reliant on the trustworthiness of a murderer. In Pichushkin's case, his haste to kill left three survivors in his wake who told police and the press every minute detail.

The first to live to tell the tale was Maria Viricheva, who was pregnant at the time of her attempted murder. Pichushkin met her in a metro station on February 23rd 2002 and must have been able to recognize that she was in pressing financial need. He crafted a story of cameras he had hidden away in a manhole in Bitsa Park, offering to sell them to her at a discount so she might turn a profit. Desperate, Maria accepted and followed him into the forest. At the opening to the sewer, Maria quickly realized her mistake as Pichushkin grabbed her and beat her head against the lid, which he then opened and dropped her inside. Miraculously, Maria maintained consciousness, and gripped the slippery walls while attempting to regain some strength amidst the freezing currents. Maria estimated that she spent almost 20 hours trapped in the sewer, struggling between trying to find a way to climb out and her fading will to live. Eventually she discovered rungs that lead to another manhole and was able to climb out to safety.

In addition to Maria, 13 year old Mikhail Lobov fell victim to Pichushkin's invitation to the park for a free drink and cigarettes. Mikhail was just one of many in a crowd of leather jackets and piercings, often hanging around the metro stations, loitering in front of food stands, and drinking. Investigators were unable to find any footage of Mikhail and Pichushkin together in the metro station nearest Bitsa Park, but they still speculate that the most likely place they met would be there. Once in the park, Mikhail's story reads like just like the others—an offer of vodka over the imaginary dog's grave, head meets manhole cover, and into the sewer he goes. The exception to the normal script comes when Mikhail's leather jacket catches on a piece of metal rather high up in the sewer, and his fall is stopped before he even reaches the water. Completely unaware, Pichushkin leaves the park thinking he killed the boy. Just moments later, Mikhail is able to crawl out shaken and disturbed, but with only minor head injuries.

Possibly the most unsettling part of these survivors' stories is when they turn to the local police to report their attacker, only to be turned away. Hospitalized and having just received news that she lost her pregnancy, Maria Viricheva frantically described the entire ordeal from beginning to end, including a full description of Pichushkin's appearance. Instead of taking action, police ignored her account and instead asked for her citizenship documentation. Maria didn't have any, and the police generously offerto ignore the whole situation, leaving her injured and alone in a hospital with Pichushkin continuing his murder spree.

When Mikhail went to police, they brushed him off as a lying punk and told him to go home. Not a month later, Mikhail ran into

Pichushkin in a crowded metro station and began yelling and pulling at his hair in frustration, dragging his attacker over to a policeman standing guard and demanding vindication. The officer escorted Mikhail out of the station and told him again just to go home. Possibly even worse is the third survivor case, of a middle aged homeless man whose story has continued to be ignored and undocumented, even in the wake of Pichushkin's conviction.

Corroborated by these detailed survivor accounts, Pichushkin's confession weaves in the rest of the story. While the sewer was serving him well for body disposal, he still wasn't getting the satisfaction he was looking for. Instead of simply using the manhole cover, Sasha escalated to bringing a yellow-handled utility hammer with him to bash in the skulls of his victims before throwing them in the sewer. At this point, around thirty people had gone missing from his neighborhood. Police still weren't interested in the goings-on of the lower class, but the local gossip had begun to gain footing and Sasha wanted credit for his work.

The Hunt for the **Bitsa Maniac**

It's not until August 15th, 2005 that the police discover their first body, deep in Bittsevsky Park. The victim was a 31 year old man named Nikolai Wirogiev, who had suffered extensive head trauma and, most shockingly, had a vodka bottle lodged in the wound. Law enforcement officer Denis Adamenko was one of the first on the scene; years later he is still able to pinpoint the exact place the first body was found, and describe the scene with gruesome detail. Though he had no idea what was in store at the time of the first police-documented murder, Adamenko would continue working on the case from the first body to Pichushkin's trial.

One month later, another man with the same injuries is found in the park. Just two weeks after that yet another body is found, and then again after only one week. Very suddenly the police began to link the murders together, realizing these stranger killings had to be the handiwork of a single killer. Though the vodka bottle signature isn't present every time, bodies begin piling up within the same age range and sex, all with substantial brain injuries. Sometimes in lieu of a vodka bottle, sticks are found in the wounds, but the reasoning for their presence remains the same: Sasha now likes to play with his victims after the fact.

Brown's interview offers some further insight into Pichushkin's newest escalation, explaining that the often-overlooked element of power is usually what creates specific signatures, such as the vodka bottle or sticks, instead of overly complex motives. "It's just that the fun ends too quickly, so instead of walking away from the body, they want to play with it because they can continue having control. *Now I'm eating you! Look at that!* It's an ongoing feeling of power."

In November of 2005 the police receive a wake up call in the form of the brutalized body and fifth victim of the unknown serial killer, a man named Nikolai Zakharchenko who was a 63 year old pensioner and an ex-cop. Like many of Pichushkin's victims, Zakharchenko lived in the same *khrushchevki* with his family, just two doors down from his murderer. Up until this point, every victim had been part of the underprivileged lower class, either homeless without family or deemed low priority by biased police. Claiming Pichushkin consciously targeted members of society that would not be missed or investigated, as some news sources allege, would be giving him far too much credit. An opportunist at heart, Sasha simply killed whenever he had the chance, with no regard for background or lack thereof, leading to the critical mistake of killing the former policeman. It's only at this point that police give the case with an accumulating body count over to an elite murder squad within the force. What the investigators don't know is that the fifth body that they've found is actually the 41st murder Sasha would later be convicted of.

By the beginning of the next year, news of a serial killer in Moscow had been upgraded from rumors among the working class to front page news. Reports from the Moscow Times warned residents of murders in Bittsevsky Park, introducing the nickname 'Bitsa Maniac' for the first time. Pichushkin's half sister Katya, who lived in the same apartment as Sasha with her husband and child, later discussed in an interview seeing a news reel about the Maniac on tv and panicking for her brother's safety. It was well known that Sasha frequented the park, but she recalls he was never afraid that there was a killer on the loose. Meanwhile, the body count continued to rise.

*A **Red Herring** in Bitsa Park*

In a fit of desperation, both the police and the general public began speculating wildly about the killer's possible identity. The investigation's gaze soon turned to the sanitarium looming suggestively on the edge of Bitsa Park. Many of the patients at the ward had privileges that included the freedom to leave the building during the day without aid, and police could not help but notice that the dumping grounds fell well within walking distance. Officers immediately restricted this freedom pending further inquiry; what began as a series of interviews eventually escalated into the interrogation of every single patient with the means to walk to the park. Eventually this branch of the investigation ceased, producing no leads or valid suspects.

By mid-February, a series of sensational rumors arose fueled purely by the area's vicious homophobia. Whispers citing evidence that never existed and eyewitness accounts simply looking for their five minutes of fame circulated not from the humble residents of the *khrushchevki,* but from the panicked upper middle class. Suddenly past visitors to the park came out of the woodwork, claiming they saw the killer fleeing through the trees and describing him as a man in women's clothing and a wig. Yet another piece of gossip spread claiming some of the bodies had been raped and found with lipstick marks all over the face, neck, and body.

Demonstrating they are not immune to the rampant homophobia and transphobia of the people they protect, local police claimed an innocent victim to their witch hunt. Late at night on February 20th, someone whom the lead investigator later described as a middle aged transvestite was seen in Bitsa Park by police canvassing the area and whose mere presence was immediately deemed suspicious.

Accounts of what followed vary greatly, with many sources glossing over the resulting exchange entirely. Claims range from the suspect attempting to flee, mysteriously breaking free of handcuffs, to pulling a knife that was never found and threatening the policemen directly. One source described nearly 200 officers being called to the scene to detain this one person. The most agreed upon and substantiated elements of that night seem to be that the suspect had a hammer in their bag, and one thing led to another that resulted in police shooting the suspect in the leg and requiring hospitalization. It was later found that their "suspect" had corroborated, air-tight alibis for each of the murders and had done nothing wrong; the hammer had been for protection against the Maniac.

*Apprehending the **Culprit***

Two months and nine bodies later, the police finally caught their break in the form of Marina Moskalyeva, the first victim since young Mikhail with direct ties to Pichushkin. Marina was a single mother to her 15 year old son and worked full time at the same grocery store as Sasha. Not only had they worked together, but when questioned after the fact, Marina's son described Pichushkin as her boyfriend and had met him before. Thanks to a subway ticket in the pocket of her jacket, police were able to easily find footage of Pichushkin meeting Marina at a metro station just outside Bitsa Park on the day of her murder. In case that had not been enough, Marina had left a note with her son saying she was going for a walk in the park, naming Sasha Pichushkin and even listing his phone number in case her son needed her.

Marina had known there was a killer at large in Bitsa Park and went anyway; likewise, Pichushkin knew Marina had left a note with his name and number, and still killed her. The man Marina knew—the shelf-stocker who lived with his mother, a man's man, a smoker and a drinker, her coworker—seemingly posed no threat. She had known him, trusted him enough to introduce him to her son. In the case of Pichushkin, investigators suggested that he craved the attention of getting caught, purposefully choosing a victim that would lead to his arrest. What seems more likely based on his confession, is that when given the opportunity to kill Sasha simply couldn't resist.

Within hours of being apprehended, Pichushkin confessed to not only Marina's murder and the twelve others the police are aware of, but claimed he had killed as many as 63 people. Plying him with sandwiches and cigarettes, detectives finally begin to understand the scope of the disappearances and consequent murders in and around the ignored *khrushchevki*. Following standard procedure for murder cases, Pichushkin is taken to the scene of the murders to reenact them on film, eventually to be used as evidence in his trial. Due to the extensiveness of his crimes, what is typically only a few hours of video continues on for nearly 40 hours filmed over the course of a month.

While Pichushkin's trial is much less of a spectacle than that of his idol, Chikatilo, it is still well publicized and attended by an aggravated crowd of his victims' families. Despite his fluctuating claims of 62 to 64 murders, the official charges brought to trial on September 13th are for 49 counts of murder and 3 attempted murders. Where police had ignored the voices of the lower class and their accounts of missing friends and families, the press steps in. With Sasha's quiet and undocumented past, journalists take statements from family members of victims, neighbors from Pichushkin's building, even random members of the community, stitching together a story for the Chessboard Killer, no matter how fabricated.

The most notable aspect of the trial was possibly the lack of controversy surrounding such a large and well-reported case. With very little deliberation, Pichushkin's psychological evaluation deemed him sane, stating that "his actions were purposeful and consistent... he was aware of what he was doing." After meeting for only three hours, the jury unanimously ruled Pichushkin guilty on all counts. Pichushkin's defense team filed an appeal within weeks but it was denied immediately. The first fifteen years of Pichushkin's life sentence were ordered to be spent in solitary confinement in a northern high security prison, where he remains today.

Despite the severity of his sentence, the prosecutors and the family of his victims are still divided in their opinions of his punishment. The chief prosecutor told the press immediately after the trial let out that he believed that "justice has been done... He received the punishment that he deserved." In contrast, Tamara Klimmova, whose husband fell victim to Pichushkin, demanded more.

"He should be handed over to the public for punishment rather than allowed to live in prison at our expense."

Now nearly nine years into his sentence, Pichushkin continues to serve out his punishment in solitary confinement. Sasha will be 44 years old when he integrates back into communal prison life, just another member of Russia's growing prison population of almost six hundred fifty thousand people, lost in the crowd of the criminal justice system.

HUSBAND KILLER : THE TRUE STORY OF WENDI ANDRIANO

46

OLIVIA WATSON

Chapter 1

A dying husband needs a devoted wife. But when love runs out, marriage becomes a burden.

On October 8, 2000, Wendi Andriano snapped. She had played the part of devoted wife to her terminally ill husband, Joe Andriano, for years, but when the love left their marriage, so did Wendi's patience for her husband's eventual demise.

Wendi had a plan to help nudge nature along, and when her plan b expired, she took matters directly into her own hands and bludgeoned him to death.

Wendi first tried to poison her husband by spiking his last meal, a homemade beef stew, with sodium azide, but Joe Andriano did not ingest enough to kill him, only enough to vomit it back up. Wendi then grabbed the nearest object, a bar stool, and beat her dying husband over the head so many times that parts of his brain became exposed.

After thinking she had successfully killed her husband twice, Wendi then realized that Joe was still breathing, so she took a knife from the family kitchen and stabbed him in the side of the throat.

Minutes later, Joe was finally dead.

This bizarre and frantic way Wendi killed her husband isn't the strangest thing about the case though. Known even to Wendi, Joe was due to die from terminal cancer within the next few years anyways.

Why Wendi couldn't wait to kill her husband is an intriguing tale wrought with sex, lies, and strangely, a lack of patience.

Chapter 2

Wendi and Joe Andriano grew up together in the small farming community of Casa Grande, Arizona. But while they both had gone to the same school, they never dated. As a minister's daughter, Wendi's social life was restricted to her father's church. Her celebration for graduating high school was even in the form of a missionary trip to Mexico in 1989. When she returned she took a job at the local clerical hospital.

Wendi met Joe in 1992 through friends. Although when the couple started dating Joe's family found the minister's daughter to be an unusual fit for the loud, outgoing former football player, they all thought she was friendly enough and approved of the match.

Joe worked for a local boat builder. He was very mechanically inclined and was a very good welder. He owned his own boat and took Wendi for several cruises around the local hot spots for speedboats. They were inseparable.

The couple married in January of 1994. Their wedding took place in a baptist church across the street from their shared elementary school. Their reception was at the Elk's club and was populated by their many friends and family. Even after two years of dating, though, Joe's family felt like they didn't know his new bride very well, but Joe seemed to be very happy, so they were happy for him.

Soon after marrying, the couple became business partners when they started a small company that did windshield repair and replacement. The business combined Wendi's office experience with Joe's mechanical experience, skills they both exceeded at, and the business thrived.

The couple hadn't been married a whole year yet before they faced their first major challenge together. That fall, Joe noticed an odd bump on his neck. When he had it tested, he was told it was a non-cancerous benign tumor, but it wasn't long before they were second-guessing the diagnoses. A year after it was removed, the tumor grew back.

A second surgery and round of tests seemed to reconfirm that the tumor was benign, but shortly after Wendi gave birth to a son in 1997, the tumor was back yet again.

The third time the tumor returned, Joe's wife and family were convinced that the tumor had to be cancer. This fear was confirmed in 1998 when Joe underwent surgery to have the bump removed for the fourth time. Joe's pre-surgery chest x-ray showed that not only was the tumor cancerous, but that the cancer had now spread across Joe's throat, chest, and lungs.

The prognosis wasn't good—Joe had a rare form of cancer and while radiation and chemotherapy were standard, there was no guarantee they would work. On top of this, Wendi was also pregnant again and was only months away from giving birth to the couple's second child.

Chapter 3

In an effort to increase Joe's chances of survival while decreasing his suffering, Wendi and Joe decided to pursue holistic treatments before resorting to chemotherapy and radiation. They had been told that chemotherapy and radiation treatments would likely not cure Joe, but they would lengthen his life by a few years; however, these years would be anything from pleasant. The horrific side-effects chemotherapy and radiation treatments cause are well known.

So the Andriano's decided first to try anything from special diets to alternative medical treatments to prayer—anything that had a chance to help Joe. Joe even attended a holistic treatment centre for cancer patients in Colorado for a few weeks where he was surrounded by other men and women facing the same prognosis as him. After seeing the bravery of others in the same position as him, Joe began thinking about his future again and began to see it as bright for the first time in a while.

After Joe returned from his holistic healing getaway with a bright new attitude, the Andriano's decided the next best step would be for Joe to begin chemotherapy treatments. He had begun to crave his future and was ready to take steps to achieve it. Unfortunately, taking these steps meant that Joe needed to quit his welding job as well as his own position in the couple's business.

To help make ends meet, Wendi returned to working for the first time since the birth of the couple's children. She ended up taking multiple jobs and worked long hours while continuing to care for her husband at home. Eventually, Wendi landed a job managing the San

Riva apartment complex in the Ahwatukee foothills, an upscale neighbourhood outside of Phoenix.

Wendi's new job came with some major perks—the salary was above average, which was nice as Wendi was now the family's breadwinner, and it required Wendi to live on site, which meant that the family now lived in a luxury apartment but paid no rent. Wendi's new job also gave her a new life. A large part of her duties as complex manager was arranging social activities for the other residents of the San Riva apartments, who were mostly young, wealthy, single businesspeople.

Every Saturday the complex hosted picnics, pool parties, or late-night socials. The residents even had their own baseball team. Wendi was required to attend every event, which meant Joe was needed to stay home with their two children. Wendi enjoyed this alone time so much that many of the residents at the San Riva had no clue she had a dying husband and two children at home. She partied like she was single.

The first few months at the San Riva went well. Wendi organized mixers and pool parties for the tenants while Joe took care of the kids. Despite being very weak from treatments, he did everything he could, he wanted to do it. He preferred to have his kids around him even when he didn't feel good.

Although they had never gotten close to their daughter-in-law, Joe's parents also pitched in with babysitting so the couple could have time alone together. They didn't get to see each other much as Wendi began spending more and more time at work. Her new job had also given her a new confidence, and she spent many nights out on the town dancing and drinking away her weekday stress with friends. Joe began to fear that Wendi would soon leave him for her new lifestyle, but this fear got sidetracked when his health continued to fail.

In the summer of 2000, when tests revealed his cancer had spread yet again, Joe and Wendi decided to increase the frequency of Joe's chemotherapy. Joe agreed to undergo more treatments, but they quickly took their toll. He lost 15 pounds in the first week alone, and Joe's doctor became concerned. It went from bad to worse very quickly.

By the beginning of October 2000, it became harder and harder to remain optimistic about Joe's chances of beating his cancer. It became apparent it was terminal, but doctors insisted that with treatment Joe could live for several more years.

No one had any idea that Joe would be dead after only the first week of the month. No one, that is, except for one person—Wendi Andriano.

Chapter 4

Just after 2:00 a.m. on October 8, Wendi Andriano called a friend who also lived in the San Riva apartment complex. She told her friend that she needed someone to stay with the kids while she took Joe to the hospital. When the friend arrived, she found Joe on the floor, barely alive.

Joe was on the floor in the fetal position. There was vomit on the floor around him and he couldn't stand up. Wendi confided in her friend that she told Joe that she had called 9-1-1 and paramedics were on the way, but this wasn't true. After seeing Joe in such poor condition, the neighbour urged Wendi to call paramedics. She then went outside to wait for them to arrive while Wendi waiting with her husband.

Wendi did call 9-1-1, but when the EMT's arrived minutes later, she refused to let them or her friend inside the apartment. She said that her husband was dying from terminal cancer and had a do not resuscitate order. Joe was not to receive any medical attention.

Just over an hour later, at 3:30 a.m., Wendi dialed 9-1-1 a second time. The same team of paramedics came to the house. It didn't take them long to realize something wasn't quite right, so they contacted the police department. Both the paramedics and the police were shocked to find out that Joe, who had been terminally ill from cancer for quite some time had died, but not from the cancer that had been slowly killing his body. He died from being repeatedly beaten with a bar stool and from being stabbed in the neck.

When the police opened the front door of the apartment, they were confronted with obvious signs of a deadly struggle. The apartment was in a complete state of disarray, and there was blood everywhere. Blood had been traced throughout the kitchen, the dining room, and the living room of the luxury apartment, and blood had spattered across the walls the ceilings. Lying in the middle of the bloody scene was Joe, with a knife wound in his neck and holes spattered across his visible skull.

While crime scene technicians surveyed the apartment, phoenix police took Wendi down to the station for a formal statement. She was wearing clothes drenched in Joe's blood and was armed with a story that explained how Joe's death had been a complete accident.

In the interrogation room, Wendi told police she and joe had spent the evening in Casa Grande visiting with Joe's parents. They put the kids to bed after they returned home, which was when Joe noticed something odd about Wendi's appearance—she wasn't wearing her wedding ring.

According to Wendi, Joe worked himself into a rage and began accusing her of having an affair. This argument turned into a shoving match, and when Joe grabbed a belt, Wendi grabbed a bar stool and swung. Joe went down on all fours so she hit him again. It was then that she called her neighbour for help. Joe may have been in a terrible state when the neighbour saw him, but according to Wendi when she went outside Joe had gotten back to his feet easily.

Wendi said she denied the EMTs access to the apartment because she and Joe were both embarrassed about the fight, but just minutes after the EMTs left, the fight got physical again.

Wendi said that her husband tried to strangle her with a telephone cord and she defended herself with the first weapon she could get in her hands—a kitchen knife. She was vague about how the knife ended up in Joe's neck though, saying she was holding the knife up when Joe suddenly fell flat on his face. The next thing she knew, blood was spurting everywhere. He must have fallen on the blade, it was simply an accident.

Many things about this story didn't make sense to the police. First of all, the timeline presented in Wendi's story didn't match the accounts of Wendi's neighbour or the EMTs. Wendi's neighbour had seen no evidence of a physical fight when they first entered the apartment—there were no broken bar stools or blood like later when the police arrived. As well, Wendi had few injuries on her body, definitely no injuries that would necessitate self defence in the form of murder.

Joe's illness also shed doubt on Wendi's story. Joe's parents told police that when the Andriano's visited earlier that evening, Joe had been so weak from his treatments that he could barely stand. They had spent the evening doting on their sick son, bringing him any comforts he wanted. If he was too weak to stand, he certainly couldn't have been strong enough to violently attack Wendi.

Police also uncovered a damning piece of evidence from Wendi herself, in a moment when she thought she was all alone. The investigators that had been questioning Wendi left her on her own in the interrogation room for some time while they fact checked some of her statements and checked in with the investigators who were scanning the crime scene for evidence. During this time, Wendi made a phone call to a coworker at the apartment complex and asked them to hide some of her files from the police. This immediately led to a search of Wendi's office where police found evidence that Wendi had in fact killed her husband. She had even been planning it for months.

Chapter 5

While both investigators strongly believed that Wendi Andriano was responsible for Joe's death, they were stumped by her motive. Why would Wendi kill her dying husband? The police didn't know, but they did have one intriguing lead—the phone call Wendi had made from the interrogation room. They were determined to find out what she was trying to hide.

When they searched her office, police discovered that Wendi had been disciplined at work for using her computer to search inappropriate items on the internet while on the clock.She had been conducting research on poisons, and how to use certain poisons to kill people. They also discovered the papers that she had tried to hide—shipping notices for a substance known as sodium azide.

Sodium azide is a lethal substance with a variety of industrial uses including propelling airbags. It is not, however, something that the average person can simply go out and buy. It's not restricted to the point where only certain companies can possess it, but it needs to be bought for a reason—something that an apartment complex didn't have. But based on the information on the shipping invoice, Wendi had found a way around that.

Wendi had created a fictitious business license using the tax ID form for the apartment complex. Using a Xerox machine and an exacto knife, Wendi had removed all information specific to the apartment complex and inserted fictitious information for a fake company.

The business name on the shipping notice was bogus, but the address wasn't. Wendi had the substance delivered to an address in Scottsdale, Arizona in an attempt to distance herself, but that plan didn't work. When the police tracked down the real address on the invoice, workers at the company positively identified Wendi as the person who had come by a couple weeks earlier to pick up a package she had mistakenly had shipped there instead of her own office.

Wendi's coworkers had seen her with a package but that she had been very mysterious with the contents. She refused to tell anyone what was inside. Had this been the sodium azide? And if so, where was it now?

Chapter 6

Suspecting that Wendi had tried to poison Joe with the sodium azide, police took samples of every medication and food they could find in the Andriano's apartment. If Joe had ingested poison, it would have explained the awful state Wendi's friend had seen him in just over an hour before he died. Luckily, the remainders of Joe's last supper, homemade beef stew, still sat in a pot on the stove.

However, police didn't find any evidence of Wendi's mysterious package, or any evidence of the sodium azide itself in Wendi and Joe's apartment. They had just begun to lose hope in finding the poison when they found out Wendi had a storage space in the building that she failed to tell the police about. Hidden behind a stack of boxes in Wendi's storage unit was a small bottle of white powder and a measuring spoon. The white powder was soon identified as sodium azide.

But the storage unit wasn't the only place investigators found the lethal substance—it was also in Joe's stomach contents and in the beef stew on the stove.

While discovering the poison helped police understand that Wendi had been trying to kill her husband, it didn't explain why she had bludgeoned him to death on October 8, 2000. Wendi had spent a lot of time researching poisons and she spent a lot of time manufacturing documents so that she could purchase the poison. It certainly wasn't a spur of the moment decision.

But why would Wendi beat and stab her husband if she had already poisoned him? Prosecutors had a theory, one that would cut to the heart of the crime. It was patience—or more precisely, Wendi's lack of it—that had killed Joe in the end.

Wendi had grown tired of waiting for the cancer to kill Joe, so she decided to give nature a little nudge by poisoning his supper. But according to the theory, when Wendi gave Joe the poison, things didn't go quite to plan. Joe hadn't ingested enough poison to kill him when he began vomiting it back up. With her plan quickly failing, Wendi panicked. She snapped.

Now improvising, Wendi beat Joe with the nearest object she could get her hands on—a bar stool. Pathologists were able to conclude that Wendi beat Joe over the head with the stool no less than twenty-four times. This beating did render Joe unconscious, but still didn't kill him so Wendi grabbed a kitchen knife and stabbed him in the part of his body that caused all this trouble in the first place—the side of his neck.

Chapter 7

Ten days after she murdered her husband, Wendi Andriano was formally charged with first degree murder. Wendi's crime was viewed as being especially cruel due to the large amount of suffering Joe had had to endure over several hours thanks to Wendi's actions. Because of this, the prosecutor's on Wendi's trial did the almost unthinkable, they sought the death penalty.

When Wendi a walked into the Arizona courtroom on September 9, 2004 she looked vastly different from the perky apartment manager that the residents of the San Riva apartments used to know.

At the time of the killing she had been blonde, she had short hair, and generally appeared to be much younger and cute than the individual who appeared in court with long dark hair and thick glasses. Previously, she had liked to look good and show her figure so her conservative dress at the trial was certainly different from the look her friends were used to seeing. She was trying to look more conservative, more innocent.

She had had plenty of time to perfect her new look—it had taken prosecutors almost four years to bring the case to trial. It had been postponed about 12 times before it was finally brought before a judge and jury.

In their opening statement, prosecutors reminded the jury that at the time of the murder Wendi had been anything but the perfect mother or wife she claimed to have been. She had been someone who had no disregard for her husband at all. While her husband was dying, she had gone out partying and started affairs, and when his condition worsened, and it began to cramp her style, she turned to poison.

Wendi didn't like her new role as family breadwinner, especially with the loss of Joe's income, and with rising medical bills, the family was in the worst financial state they had ever been in. Wendi had thought she was going to be able to be a stay-at-home-mom for the rest of her life, and she did not adjust well to her return to the workforce. So Wendi had found an out.

Although Joe did not have any life insurance, even though Wendi had asked several friends to pretend to be Joe in medical exams so he could be insured, Joe had filed a malpractice suit against his former doctor who had continually told him his tumor was benign when it was in fact spreading throughout his body. If Joe died and the lawsuit went through, Wendi would likely walk away with a multi-million dollar settlement.

More than money though, Wendi had wanted freedom. She wanted the freedom to be single again, she wanted freedom to the ball-and-chain who was slowly dragging her spirit into his grave along with himself. Wendi wanted to not have to care about her dying husband anymore, who was too weak to provide her with any love.

Wendi maintained her plea of innocence throughout the trial, and her defence team attempted to prove she had been the victim of abuse not only on the night of Joe's death but also throughout the couple's entire marriage. To explain the poison, Wendi told the court that Joe had been the one who had grown tired of waiting for the cancer to end his life, and had asked Wendi to help him do it himself.

On the witness stand Wendi said that Joe had willingly taken the poison, but she also stuck by the story that she had originally told police, that Joe had suspected an affair and became enraged when she affirmed them. He became deranged and attacked her, starting the bloody fight. Wendi claimed Joe had died during the ensuing struggle.

Wendi's story wasn't enough to convince the court though, and on November 18, 2004 she was found guilty of the crime. It had taken the jury only two-and-a-half-hours to come to its unanimous decision. Six years after her husband joe had been diagnosed with terminal cancer, Wendi Andriano faced a possible death sentence of her own.

On December 20, 2004, the jurors assigned to Wendi Andriano's case met and decided on Wendi's fate—it would be death for Ms Andriano. Wendi, along with most of the courtroom, was aghast. Even Joe's family was shocked by the decision. Wendi Andriano became the second ever woman to be put on death row in Arizona, a state that reserves the death penalty for the worst of the worst.

Wendi Andriano has since attempted to appeal the court's decision, but as of early 2017, all attempts have been denied and Wendi continues to wait on death row. Wendi and Joe's children now live with Joe's parents, who continue to mourn the loss of their beloved son.

Joe Andriano's death was especially long, and especially cruel, but no happy ending was found when Wendi was sentenced to her own death. Many view the conclusion of this case to be the saddest possible outcome. On October 8, 2000, two lives were lost, and two children were left without parents.

THE JUST DO IT KILLER

SARAH THOMPSON

McCamey, Texas. A town of less than two thousand people, out in the scorching Texas desert, where downtown is a stretch of black road with marginally more buildings on either side. McCamey is the type of town that lies, more or less, entirely forgotten by the rest of the United States, down in the deep heat of Texas. It was in McCamey, in 1940, that Gary Mark Gilmore was born. Gilmore would have, perhaps, gone one to live and die a completely unnoticed life if circumstances had been different. As it stands, Gary Mark Gilmore would gain fame through his life for being the first person sentenced to death in the United States in nearly ten years for the crimes that he committed.

On December 4th, in 1940, Frank and Bessie Gilmore became the parents of their second son, Gary Mark Gilmore. Frank and Bessie were married on a whim, and Frank was said to have other wives and families that he otherwise ignored. Bessie was a Mormon from Provo, Utah, but she had been outcast by her community. Bessie and Frank met and married in California, but the both of them eventually moved to McCamey, Texas, where Gary Mark had been born. Gilmore would have three brothers: Frank Jr., Gaylen and Mikal Gilmore. It was in McCamey that Frank and Bessie were living with their first son Frank Jr., and existing under the false name of "Coffman" in order to escape detection from law enforcement. When he was born, Gary Mark Gilmore had been given the name Faye Robert Coffman - Faye, named after Frank Gilmore Sr.'s mother, Fay.

However, the name Faye Robert didn't stick. His mother, Bessie, decided to change it to Gary Mark Gilmore after they left Texas. Moving wasn't uncommon for the Gilmore family. Gary spent most of his childhood moving from city to city throughout most of the Western United States, along with this three brothers and his parents. Frank Gilmore supported the family during this time with the sale of fraudulent magazine subscriptions. Gary's relationship with his father was rocky, as was the rest of the family's relationship with Frank Gilmore, Sr. He was described as a man with a quick temper, and who was easily angered. He was also a strict father, and one to dole out corporal punishment when and if he saw fit. Frank often did not need a reason to beat his sons, and would routinely whip them with a razor strop, belt or whip.

Frank Gilmore, Sr. did not only take out his anger and violence on his sons. Though this was less frequent, he would also take to beating Bessie. The relationship between Frank and Bessie was also volatile. Gary grew up in a household in which his parents would often take to screaming at one another, and verbally abusing one another with insults and digs at each other's religions. Bessie would even threatened to kill Frank Sr. some nights. The two parental figures of the household were constantly at one another's throats, and it was the source of a lot of distress and frustration and turmoil within the Gilmore family.

Exposure to violence between his mother and father and the crimes of his father did nothing for Gary's disposition.

While his other brothers seemed to escape the thrall of their household unscathed, Gary wasn't so lucky. There's no telling what a calmer household would have done for Gary, and if his rocky home life was the root cause for the crimes he would commit and the path he would soon begin to take in life.

Despite the Gilmore family's nomadic lifestyle for the greater part of Gary's children, they finally settled down in Portland, Oregon in the year 1952. Gary was twelve at the time, and like most twelve year olds, he was starting to stretch his legs and discover some semblance of independence and self-identity. During his adolescence, Gary was incredibly intelligent. He tested an IQ score of 133, and throughout his schooling career he tested and scored well on both aptitude and achievement tests. Gary even showed an incredible ability for artistic talent. He was on the entirely right track to being a successful student and graduating from school.

Unfortunately, Gary did not continue down this path. He was in the ninth grade when he decided to drop out of high school. It was then that Gary became caught up in petty crimes, and took to anti-social behaviors. After he dropped out of high school, Gary ran away from home with a friend. They traveled from Oregon all the way down to Texas. There they stayed for several months before finally returning back to Portland. It was at 14 that he finally managed to succumb to his first arrest. He had started a car theft ring with some friends. Rather than put him in jail, law enforcement released him back to his father and all Gary received from police was a slap on the wrist and a warning to keep in line.

Gary didn't take either the warning or the gift seriously. It wasn't any more than two weeks later when Gary found himself back in court on yet another charge for car theft. At this point, the court sent Gary to the MacLaren Reform School for Boys. The MacLaren Reform School was a correctional facility located in Woodburn, Oregon. The boys residing in MacLaren were anywhere from age 13 to 25, and had committed and range of crimes. In retrospect, due to Gary's immense intelligence and his own willful nature, it might have been the fact that he was sent to MacLaren that had redoubled his affinity for crime, or at least his unwillingness to stop.

Gary was released the next year from MacLaren, but he didn't stay out for long. For the next several years, Gary would be in and out of prison for various crimes. In 1960, at 20 years old, Gary was convicted of another car theft. This time, he was sentenced to time in the Oregon State Correctional Institute. He served a minimal amount of time there, and was even released later in the year. It was around this time in 1961, that Gary's father, Frank Gilmore Sr., was diagnosed with lung cancer. It was terminal. Gary's tumultuous relationship with his father was coming to an end.

In 1962, Gary was once more arrested. This time, the crime was much more severe than stealing a car. He was charged with armed robbery and assault, and was sentenced to Oregon State Penitentiary. It was during this stint in prison that Frank Gilmore Sr. passed away from lung cancer. Gary was in prison at the time and was unable to say goodbye, or even receive the news directly from his family. One of the guards that the Oregon State Penitentiary gave Gary the news about his father's passing.

Gary's relationship with his father had never been good. He grew up in a household where his father and mother were always at odds, with him and his brother's caught in the middle. Frank Gilmore, Sr. was brutal, violent and strict on his sons. He went beyond disciplining them when he raised his belt or whip against Gary and his brothers. Mikal had even once described their father as a "cruel and unreasonable man". And yet, despite all of that - despite the years spent moving around at the whim of his con man father, and despite the years spent at the end of a leather strop and watching his father beat his mother, Gary Gilmore was distraught over the old man's death. When he was given the news of Frank Sr.'s passing, Gary tried to end his life by slitting his wrists.

The suicide attempt was unsuccessful, and Gary Gilmore remained alive. He was eventually released back into suicide. For two years, Gary either stayed out of trouble or managed not to get caught. And yet, in 1964, Gary was once more returned to prison - on the charges of armed robbery and assault, once more. This time, Gary was sentenced to fifteen years in prison for his habitual offenses. A prison psychiatrist finally diagnosed Gary with antisocial personality disorder as well as something called intermittent psychotic decompensation. Psychotic decompensation is a term that describes the rapid deterioration of someone's mental health that they had been, up until then, been otherwise maintaining. This, along with Gary's personality disorder characterized by his disregard and often violation of other people's rights and autonomy, make him a perfect package for crime.

By the time he was 30, Gary Gilmore had spent the greater part of his adult life in and out of prison. The intelligence that had heard him such high marks and a promising future when he was a boy didn't disappear over the years. In fact, Gary used much of his time in prison to write poetry and make artwork. It was these talents that initially won Gary conditional release to a halfway house in Eugene, Oregon. In 1972, he was granted permission to live weekdays at the halfway house under the condition that he stay out of trouble and take art classes at the local community college. However, in line with Gary's usual behavior, he ended up never registering for classes at the community college. Within a month of his initial conditional release, Gary Gilmore couldn't resist the siren call of crime, and was once more arrested and convicted on the charge of armed robbery.

Gary Gilmore's behavior in prison turned from quiet poetry crafting to violence, and he was eventually transferred to a maximum-security federal prison in Marion, Illinois. He was transferred there in 1975. Now 35, it was looking like Gary Gilmore would be spending many more years of is still short life in prison. While he was serving his time in Marion, Gary began writing letters with his cousin, Brenda Nicol. Perhaps it was through Gary's particular intelligence that he manipulated her into believing he deserved a second change, or maybe it was Brenda's own idea. All the same, in 1976, Gary was once more given conditional release into the care of his cousin, Brand. He would live with her in Provo, Utah, under the condition that he stay out of trouble. Brenda would help him look for work and aid in his reform, offering Gary a support system that he had not had previously.

Gary began working at a shoe repair store owned by his uncle, Vern Damico. He also worked, briefly, for an insulation company. This rehabilitation seemed to be on the up and up, and Gary's life was being steered clear of all his previous habits. Unfortunately, Gary wasn't able to keep away from his old ways for long. Soon after his foray into a new life, Gary was back into his old habits of drinking, stealing and fighting. He got into a relationship with a 19 year old woman by the name of Nicole Baker. Nicole was both a window and a divorcee and she had two young children at the time that she and Gary got together. Their relationship was casual at first, but it didn't take long for things between Gary and Nicole to become both intense and strained. Perhaps it was from his own parent's relationship that Gary had learned how to interact with others in a romantic sense - that is, he didn't learn very well at all.

Gary soon began imitate his father. He became controlling with Nicole, and threatening. Their relationship was strained both from Gary's violent behavior, as well as pressure from Nicole's family for her to leave him. Gary was having trouble adjusting to life outside of prison, after spending nearly half of his life, and almost all of his adult life, behind bars. His relationship with Nicole was just a precursor to Gary's inevitable inability to reform himself and stay the straight and narrow path.

It all came to a head on July 19th, 1976. Gary Gilmore stopped at a gas station in Orem, Utah. He had been travelling at the time with April, Nicole Baker's younger sister. During this time, Gary and Nicole were still off-again on-again, in an unstable and volatile relationship. It was around 10:30 in the evening that Gary stopped and told April that he needed to make a phone call. He left April in the car and entered the gas station. It was there that he robbed the gas station attendant, Max Jensen, at gunpoint, continuing his affinity for armed robbery. This time, however, Gary took it another step. After Gary had instructed Jensen to give him the money box, he forced him into the bathroom and had him lay down on the floor. Max Jensen obeyed all of Gary's demands, but his obedience was for naught. According to Gary's confession of the crime, he held his gun against Jensen's head and said, "This one is for me," before firing the gun once. He then stated, "For Nicole", before firing the gun a second time, shooting Jensen twice and then leaving him, dead and bleeding, on the bathroom floor of the gas station.

Leaving Orem behind, Gary traveled back to Provo with April and spent the night in a motel nearby where he left his truck in a service garage to be repaired. The evening after his armed robbery and murder in Orem, Gary robbed a hotel manager by the name of Ben Bushnell, who lived on the property with his family. Much like the victim before him, Ben Bushnell complied with every one of Gary's demands. An eyewitness, motel guest Peter Arroyo, would later describe Gary ordering Bushnell to lie on the floor. Much like Jensen, Bushnell was shot and killed. When he tried to dispose of his weapon that he used in both robberies and murders, Gary managed to accidentally shoot himself in his right hand. Had he not, he might have managed to get away with both killings and continue on to commit more escalated violence. As it were, his bleeding hand alerted the garage mechanic, Michael Simpson, who had seen Gary trying to hide the gun in the nearby bushes.

Michael Simpson wrote down Gary's license plate number after hearing about a shooting at a nearby motel on a police scanner. He called the police and alerted them of the goings on, of Gary's wounded hand and of his disposing of the gun in the bushes by the mechanic garage. Meanwhile, Gary had called his cousin for support, but she was unsympathetic to his plight. She called the police as well, and Gary was taken into custody after law enforcement found him at the edge of town not long after the incident.

Gary Mark Gilmore isn't the most prolific killer in history, or even of his time. He probably wouldn't even be classified as a serial killer, or even a spree killer. It's Gary's particular circumstances that make him so famous, however. It was the same year that Gary Mark Gilmore was arrested for two counts of murder that the U.S Supreme Court upheld a series of new death penalty statutes in the court decision of Gregg v. Georgia. Before that, death penalty statutes had been deemed "cruel and unusual punishment", and therefore deemed unconstitutional. It wasn't until the 1976 Supreme Court decision that the death penalty was reinstated. Perhaps, if this ruling had not occurred, Gary Mark Gilmore would have rotted away in life in prison as many others had before him during the time where the death penalty was not in effect. Gary Mark Gilmore was charged with both the murders of Jensen and Bushnell, though only Bushnell's murder actually went to trial, due to a lack of evidence and eyewitnesses to Jensen's murder—even though Gary admitted to both.

He was held in custody until October 5th, 1976. It was on that day that Gary Mark Gilmore's trail began in Provo. It lasted only two days. Unhappy with his lawyers' lack of cross-examination and lack of their own witnesses for his defense, Gary persuaded the judge to let him take the stand in his own defense. He claimed dissociation and lack of control, and tried to make a case of insanity. His own attorney's called four separate psychiatrists to shoot down this attempt of claiming insanity, showing that Gary had full control and awareness of what he was doing during the crimes. Not even his antisocial personality disorder was enough for him to actually meet the legal definition of insanity. Despite his intelligence and his skilled manipulation tactics, Gary was not able to present a defense for himself. It seemed that he knew when he was beat.

On October 7, 1976, after two days of trial, the jury returned a guilty verdict. They also agreed on the death penalty, due to circumstances surrounding Gary's crimes. This would be the first execution in the United States in ten years, and the first execution that would happen after the Supreme Court decision to allow the death penalty once more.

Gary's mother, Bessie, attempted to sue to for a stay of execution, despite the fact that Gary himself chose not to pursue habeas corpus. In a unanimous decision, the U.S Supreme Court refused to even hear Bessie's claim, and her son was slated to be executed. A death penalty sentence in modern times includes lethal injection, as it has been proven to be the most humane way of sentencing a criminal to death, unlike the methods of the past such as hanging or the electric chair. During Utah in 1976, however, the only methods available for executions were hanging, or a firing squad. Gary Mark Gilmore had already accepted his fate as the first man to be executed in the United States in almost ten years. To Gary, a hanging had room for error. He told the court, "I prefer to be shot," and chose the firing squad. Thus, his execution was set for 8 am on November 15th.

Despite having accepted his fate, Gary ended up actually receiving a few stays of execution, though he did not seek them out and explicitly did not want them. It was at the hands of the American Civil Liberties Union (ACLU) and his attorneys that drew out his already chosen execution. When his lawyers tried to call of an appeal on his case, Gary opted instead to fire them. He was ready to face his death, and he saw no reason to draw it out any longer. It was this refusal of appeal that drew the ACLU's attention. The ACLU made efforts, hand in hand with the National Association for the Advancement of Colored People to turn over Gary's execution. However, it wasn't entirely for Gary's benefit. They were using Gary's case to benefit the prisoners who were standing on death row throughout the United States, all of whom were now in danger of facing execution now that the Supreme Court had reinstated the death penalty.

Gary's execution got tied up in legalities. He was ready for it to all be over. In November 1976, while Gary was taking part in a Board of Pardons hearing, Gary said this of all the legal attempts to spare his life: "It's been sanctioned by the courts that I die and I accept that." The dragged out legal battle between the courts and the ACLU put off Gary's execution for months, and in the interim Gary attempted suicide twice. His first attempted occurred on November 16th when his first stay of execution was announced. Nicole Barrett visited Gary in prison, despite her having broken off their relationship. They kissed and held one another during Nicole's visit, and the reason for it became clear. Nicole had snuck in sleeping pills. After she had left, Gary swallowed the overdose of pills—while at the same time, miles away in her own home, Nicole Barrett had done the same, the both of them attempting suicide. Gary had not taken enough sleeping pills for the dosage to be fatal. Nicole took a larger dosage of sleeping pills, which resulted in her slipping into a coma for several days. Gary was not finished with attempting to end his life. With or without Nicole, Gary attempted suicide again one month later to the exact day in December. When that didn't work, he took up a hunger strike.

Finally, Gary was given a date for execution: January 17th, 1977. On the night before his execution, Gary requested that he be allowed to have an all-night gathering that consisted of his friends and family. He was granted the request, and spent his last evening surrounded by the people in his life that could be considered his loved ones. Gary's last meal consisted of potatoes and steak to eat, and milk and coffee to drink. For whatever reason, Gary didn't touch his steak and potatoes. The last thing that he had was the milk and the coffee. The next morning, on January 17th, Gary's last stay of execution was overturned at 7:30 AM, and Gary was finally allowed to go through with his execution as he had wanted so many months previously.

At 8:07 AM, Gary was taken behind the prison to an abandoned cannery. He was placed and secured into a chair with a wall of sandbags behind him for the purpose of absorbing the bullets. In tradition of firing squad, five local police were placed behind a cloth with only a small hole for them to put through the barrel of their rifles, aimed directly at his body from 20 feet away. In Utah tradition, the firing squad consists of four men with live rounds and one man with a blank round. This is done, ostensibly, so that the men comprised of the firing squad will never know which one of them fired the killing shot.

When he was asked for any last words, all Gary Mark Gilmore had to say was this: "Let's do it!" A black hood was placed on his head, and the five gunmen were allowed to fire a single bullet into the body of the first man to undergo execution in the United States in almost ten years. Gary's youngest brother, Mikal Gilmore, was allowed to inspect the clothes worn by his brother after his execution. Allegedly, there were five holes left in the clothes, not four. He noted this in his memoir, 'Shot in the Heart', and mused that Utah wanted to take no chances on leaving his brother alive. Mikal's memoir goes in depth into his relationship with Gary, as well as the strained relationship he had with his family, as well as the aftermath of his own brother's execution at the hands of the state of Utah.

Before his death, Gary had requested that his organs be donated to those in need of transplant. Because of his death by firing squad, it can be presumed that some of his internal organs were useless, now riddled with bullet holes - mainly, his heart, where a piece of black cloth had been pinned as a target for the firing squad. Strangely enough, though, two people were able to receive corneal transplants, courtesy of now famed murderer Gary Mark Gilmore. After his autopsy, Gary's body was cremated. In a grandiose decision by his family, Gary's ashes were then scattered from an airplane over Spanish Fork, Utah.

Gary Mark Gilmore is notorious, perhaps not for his crimes, but for when his crimes occurred. He would have otherwise rotted away in prison, unknown but for the people whose lives he had touched, no matter how horrid and terrible that touch may be. It was by virtue of the place and time that he had committed his crimes that gained Gary Mark Gilmore his fame of being the first man executed in the United States since the death penalty had been reinstated. It is more than just those who were involved in his case and legal battles that remember his name. Gary Mark Gilmore is now known for his own battle for execution. He is remembered in both the minds of those involved, as well as the legal histories of the United States.

The Killer of South Lake City

James Foster

75

Ronnie Lee Gardner

Ronnie Lee Gardner was an American criminal- not a serial killer, but a notorious murderer. His first murder, a robbery gone wrong, was nothing to hit nationwide headlines. But his numerous escape attempts, in particular the way in which he escaped, grabbed the attention of the mainstream media back in the 1980's. Since then, his story was one of constant parole hearings and unsuccessful appeals against the death sentence he had been handed down.

Ronnie Lee Gardner's story is a sad one: not just because of the deaths of his innocent victims, or of his own life, precious like all life, which he wasted in robbery, drugs and crime from the days of his youth. But his story is a sad one because his life, so fraught with physical and sexual abuse, poverty and institutionalization could have been so much different. While his crimes overshadow any sympathy that his awful life could possibly garner, it is nonetheless instructive to look at how things went so wrong for him, and perhaps to understand how criminals become what they are.

Ronnie Lee Gardner's early life

Gardner's crimes were undeniable. Cold blooded and merciless, Ronnie rightfully earned a reputation as one of America's most deplorable criminals, and eventually ended up on death row. There's more about that later, but before we think about Ronnie's later life, it would be good for us trying to understand his crimes and us as a larger society to think about his early life too- and how he became who he became.

Ronnie was born in Salt Lake City, Utah. Like his family and neighbours, he was raised as a member of the Church of Latter Day Saints, and would remain a Mormon his entire life. He was the youngest child of Dan and Ruth Gardner, who had six more besides Ronnie. Ruth had two more from a previous relationship. But Dan was a frequent and heavy drinker, and the couple's marriage was anything but happy. Dan couldn't hold down a job for any amount of time, both he and Ruth were violent to one another and to their children, and spent more time drunk or high than working or caring for their kids.

They split when Ronnie was only eighteen months old. Normally the adage is that a child will be better off with two separated, but happy, parents rather than a couple that 'stay together for the children' even though they're miserable. But Ronnie held a bad hand either way. Six months after the divorce, Ronnie was taken into care. He had been found wandering the streets alone- a toddler of two years- while his mother got high. Presumably because of a failure on the part of Utah's social services, Ruth was deemed a fit mother and Ronnie was returned to her- even though he was malnourished and was clearly not cared for.

At around the same time, Ruth was remarried to a man named Bill Lucas, who was no better than Dan. He was incarcerated at the time. On her own, Ruth was anything but capable of looking after her children, and they did as they pleased all day, every day. Few made the effort to go to school- why would you, when you can go and do what you want all day? It's a childhood fantasy that almost everyone wished for, but the reality is grim and shocking rather than fun. Ronnie was regularly beaten and abused by his parents and siblings and was scrawny, malnourished and dirty his entire childhood.

Because of Ruth's carefree lifestyle, Ronnie was left to be raised by his older siblings. The family moved away from Salt Lake City when Ronnie was four, although little changed, and Ronnie would later tell social workers and his lawyers that he had been sexually abused from a very young age by an older brother, and an older sister and her friend when he was five. At age six, another brother had introduced him to sniffing glue, and at age ten he was smoking cannabis. He dropped out of school in the fourth grade, which was the last state education Ronnie would ever receive; he would later be schooled at detention centers, but of course, it's not the same.

Ronnie was a frequent shoplifter, and acted as lookout for his stepdad during burglaries. Ronnie and his brother Randy stole some cowboy boots from a store when the former was still just ten years old, and the paid were arrested and sent to a juvenile detention center. The authorities called the boys' father Dan, who for whatever reason decided to leave Ronnie but take Randy home. Any of this would be enough to severely scar a child, let alone all of this; and it would be enough to write off an adult, let alone a child. But believe it or not, this was far from the end of Ronnie's awful childhood.

A year later, Ronnie was committed by his parents to Utah State Hospital. They had sent him there because they felt he was overactive- which he was- but the doctors at Utah State felt that his home life was so dysfunctional that he would be far better off living in a mental institution. One of the doctors commented that at the age of eleven, he had the bone structure and strength of a five year old; Dr. Craig Haney, a psychology professor who would later testify at one of Ronnie's many hearings before the Utah Board of Pardons and Parole, told them that his parents had completely given up on caring for him in any way, shape or form.

By the age of 11, he had been in detention twelve times in a number of different institutions. He attended Utah State Industrial School, a juvenile detention center, where he was again sexually abused- and after he left the school aged fourteen, he ran away from home to live with the man who had abused him, who was appointed his foster parent. Soon after, he met the woman who became his wife, and had two children when he was aged 16 and 19. When his second child was born, he was in prison having been convicted of robbery; and this is when his later 'career' can be said to have begun in earnest.

He escaped from the maximum security unity of Utah State Prison in 1981, a year after his son was born, but was not long after found and sent back. He escaped custody again when he was taken to University of Utah Hospital after faking illness- during the course of which, he beat a man so badly that he needed reconstruction surgery to his face. Gardner had a long history of escape: from being found wandering alone at the age of two onwards, he had hated staying at home- for obvious reasons- and had taken any and all opportunities to run away. His mother and stepfather didn't care, and preferred him gone. They couldn't deal with his 'hyperactivity' and didn't like him being around the house.

The point of introducing Gardner like this, rather than simply listing his crimes, is not to say that he was the victim of his circumstances, or necessarily to elicit sympathy; but it is hard to imagine how anybody could have grown up in such an environment and gone on to have a long and happy life, with a successful career, a strong marriage and a happy family. Ronnie's path had been set from the start to take a turn into a dark and depressing criminal world; how it could have gone any other way is an impossible question to answer.

What did Ronnie do?

Ronnie escaped from the University of Utah Hospital on August 6th, 1984. It was only two months later that he was in trouble again- but this time, rather than either getting away with his robbery, or getting caught red handed, the robbery went wrong. This time, Ronnie chose to rob the Cheers Tavern in Salt Lake City. During the robbery, he shot the bartender, Melvyn John Otterstrom, straight to the head, to the face. Whether Otterstrom put up a fight or tried to stop Ronnie somehow was never firmly established.

As for the point of the robbery, it was a straight cash grab; although Gardner stood to gain less than $100 from what was left at the end of the night. Gardner had been under the influence of cocaine at the time. He wasn't immediately apprehended; the case remained open for three weeks before a tip revealed that Gardner was the likely murderer. In a bizarre twist, Gardner had attended the funeral of the man he murdered and claimed to be a childhood friend.

The entirety of the evidence and testimony pointed to Gardner's guilt, and the outcome of the trial was all but a certainty. In his defence, Gardner said that Otterstrom had put up a fight, but again, no evidence was found to corroborate what he said. According to the ballistics reports, the victim had been lying down on the ground, on his back, and Gardner had pointed the gun straight at him and shot him, clean through the head. How exactly the defence planned to make a case that Otterstrom had put up a fight was unclear, but Gardner would nonetheless claim so during trial. At this point, the murder was local news, but it was what happened next that drew the attention that made Gardner famous across America.

On April 2nd of 1985, Gardner made an escape attempt using a revolver that was smuggled to him as he walked along a public hallway in the Metropolitan Hall of Justice in Salt Lake City. He obtained it as he was being escorted into the courthouse from the underground parking lot- it was handed to him by an unknown woman, although she was later arrested. Gardner was immediately shot by the guard escorting him, Luther Hensley, but not fatally; Gardner tried to shoot back, and hit an unarmed bailiff named George Kirk.

It was policy for guards such as Luther Hensley to shoot to kill in situations such as these, and later, Salt Lake County Sheriff N.D. Hayward said that Hensley should have done so. However, a review of the available evidence concluded that Gardner had used hostages as human shields during his escape attempt, and prevented any guard from getting a clear shot. This all pointed to a very well planned escape attempt, rather than an opportunistic dash for freedom. But having managed to get his gun, and being able to run, run is what Gardner did. But he found the exits impassable, and so was forced to stay in the courthouse for the time being.

He was cornered in the courtroom archives and confronted by two attorneys- Robert Macri and Michael Burdell. Threatening them both, Gardner fatally shot Burdell, who had been doing *pro bono* work at the court. Gardner swiftly ran outside, but found himself surrounded by a dozen or more police officers, all of them armed. Dressed in his maximum security prison whites, manacled and with a chain around his waist, Gardner was stood in a standoff with the officers: they ordered him to put the gun down, but he would not.

After around a minute, he decided that there was no way he could escape this time. He threw the gun away, and told the officers not to hurt him; he was bleeding copiously from the bullet wound in his chest at this point. The officers ordered him to lie down, and took him back into custody, but were forced to take him to the same University of Utah Health Sciences Center that he had escaped from before, because of his wounds. George Kirk, the unarmed bailiff that Gardner shot, was taken to hospital at the same time, but unfortunately died later that same day.

Shortly after the shooting, an extensive search of the courthouse was conducted to search for evidence, or clues as to who may have tried to help Gardner escape. During that search, a duffel bag full of men's clothing was found in the women's restroom, and using this evidence, they tracked down and took Darcy Perry McCoy into custody-Gardner's getaway driver for the robbery gone wrong a year before, who had actually gone on to testify against him. Carma Jolley Hainsworth, Darcy's sister, was eventually sentenced to eight years in prison for attempting to help Gardner escape, and having provided the bag of clothes and concocted the plan.

Gardner was already potentially facing the death penalty for the murder of Otterstrom, but his escape attempt and the further carnage and deaths he caused tipped the scales. In June of that same year, Gardner pleaded guilty to Otterstrom's murder, and was sentenced to life in prison; his further trial was held later in 1985, and in that case, the jury deliberated for less than three hours to find him guilty of capital murder. For this charge, Gardner was sentenced to death, for which he chose the firing squad rather than lethal injection.

Very few people have been executed by firing squad in the United States in the recent past. In fact, only two other than Ronnie have chosen the option since 1976; and we are unlikely to see any more, as states increasingly deny prisoners the option. Utah actually outlawed the firing squad long before Ronnie was executed in 2010, but since he had already chosen the option before it was outlawed in 2004, it was still available to him. The only other two prisoners to die by firing squad have been Gary Gilmore and John Albert Taylor. Gardner was later quoted as saying that he liked the firing squad because there was no possibility of mistakes, and less pain than the electric chair or- as is sometimes evident- through the lethal injection.

Gardner's time in prison

Gardner was imprisoned from 1985 onwards, since before he was sentenced to death, because of his guilt in the Offerman case. Time and time again, Gardner made life difficult for the guards holding him and the prison system containing him. In 1987, he and a number of fellow prisoners forced a hearing where they claimed they had been treated unfairly, in 'unsanitary conditions' and with low quality food. Gardner and his friends filed nine separate complaints that they were kept in conditions of 'unconstitutional confinement', although nothing came of it.

A review of his life in the *Salt Lake Tribune* written shortly before Gardner's death contained an interesting story. In 1987, Gardner broke the glass partition between prisoners and visitors while he and other inmates barricaded the doors, so that he and the woman visiting him could have sex. While drunk on alcohol he had fermented himself in his sink in 1994, Gardner stabbed a fellow inmate using a shiv he fashioned from a pair of sunglasses, almost killing him.

In fact, this episode almost landed Gardner yet another charge of a capital crime, because of a little-used law in Utah which could be used to condemn prisoners for attacking and killing their fellow inmates. The law was almost never used, especially because it solely applied to inmates who had been sent to prison for first degree felonies already. As for how this law could result in the death penalty- which was what the prosecution were seeking- there was no precedent in

United States law. Because of the outdated nature of the law and its very limited application, Gardner's case was thrown out and the law itself overturned. Either way, the inmate that Gardner attacked eventually survived.

In terms of his appeals, Gardner was actually egged on by his attorneys rather than determined to prove his 'innocence'. At least three times throughout the whole process, he told his attorneys that he didn't want to carry on, but was convinced to keep going. He was in near-solitary confinement during the majority of his time in prison, and suffered from a number of ailments like rheumatoid arthritis, hepatitis C and leukemia. His appeal continued right up until the point of his execution- in fact, it was the only thing delaying his death.

During his final hearings, Gardner asked the board to reduce his sentence from capital punishment to life without parole; part of his argument was that his children had, since his incarceration, made him a grandfather. He had also made friends, including one Robert Macri, who he had threatened during his escape attempt all those years ago. According to both Macri and Gardner, Macri had begun visiting him in prison, and had taught him grammar and history- and yoga.

At the hearings, which took place on June 10th 2010, his attorneys argued that the meningitis he had contracted while still a child had given him brain damage, and that in conjunction with the glue sniffing he had done since an early age, that he could not be fully held responsible for his actions. This had been an argument that he and his defence had used back in the original trial, but without much success; it seemed as if they had few options, especially since he was so obviously guilty of the crimes, and that the crimes carried the obvious penalty of death.

In the meantime, Gardner had had an idea for how he would like to live his life, if he were allowed to live it. Of course, he conceded that the rest of his life *would* be behind bars; there was nothing he could do about that, no matter how much he appealed. But after reading a book about gardening, Gardner had an idea about a farm: an organic farm that he could set up through his brother, with the aim of helping troubled kids.

After all of his years with no guidance, Gardner felt that he could help guide youths away from a life of drugs and crime, and into a 'chemical free' and happy life. Whether the 'plan' was anything but a ploy to try and convince the board to overturn his death penalty, we can never know; but the plan was between him, his brother and extended family, and his attorney Tyler Ayres who was helping to finance it. Even if it was a ploy, it was a genuine one, and would have genuinely helped young people.

He had even been in touch with celebrities like Oprah Winfrey in an attempt to secure funding for it, and his attorney backed up his client by saying that his was a genuine wish to help young people escape the life that he couldn't ever get out of. Of course, we won't ever know now. Ronnie's final appeal was rejected, which paved the way to his execution. It had been twenty five years since his initial incarceration, and there were no more hurdles left for the state to face to finally put him to death.

Ronnie's execution

Because of Ronnie's unique story, and the fact that he was going to become the first man to die by firing squad in the United States for fourteen whole years, his execution was attended by nine media witnesses- one of whom, Nate Carlisle, wrote his first hand account for the Salt Lake Tribune. In it, he described both the scene and the man about to die.

Perhaps what you imagine is a man stood up against a wall, perhaps facing his killers, or perhaps with his back to them and his hands up. But Ronnie was strapped to a chair, and his head was covered by a black hood- perhaps easily mistaken for a man about to become the victim of an electric chair. He was restrained by the wrists and ankles with thick, padded belts, and as if that weren't enough, he was held back by more belts around his shoulders and waist. His head was strapped in place, again like the victim of an electric chair.

The chair on which he sat was propped up on a small wooden platform almost like a miniature stage. To his left and to his right stood two tall piles of sandbags, for any stray bullets that for some reason the marksmen managed to send wide- although quite how they could miss a man strapped to a chair and unable to even see them, perhaps apart from a last minute change of heart, is difficult to say. Behind the chair was a small wooden wall, and the whole apparatus was painted in a dark shade of black, befitting of such a sombre occasion as an execution.

Carlisle described how Gardner was dressed in a standard issue blue prison jumpsuit, the arms folded up past his elbow, revealing his tattoos. While he waited to die, his fists were clenched and his chin and head firmly held high. Carlisle and his eight fellow journalists were penned into their own special viewing area behind a six foot wide bulletproof window. What they could see of the room was sparse: the cinder block walls, the floor and the ceiling were all white. There was no décor.

When Gardner's hood was removed, and the curtain in front of the watching journalists' window was drawn back, Carlisle was shocked by what he saw. First, Gardner 'looked nothing like the athletic 23-year-old with the red hair who murdered Melvyn Otterstrom in a robbery, nor did he flash that grin that defined those infamous photographs of him shackled on the courthouse lawn after killing Michael Burdell and wounding Nick Kirk in 1985.'

Instead, he looked like 'Utah's own ghost of Hannibal Lecter'. He was as white as a sheet, something which Carlisle pointed out was only emphasised by the black chair and background behind him. He was completely bald, with only a shock of hair, a goatee on his chin. Because of his restraints, Ronnie couldn't move an inch- even his head, which meant that he could do nothing but stare forward towards the men about to shoot him. Hanging over his left shoulder was a small target, only 2 inches by 2 inches, placed carefully over his heart. The shooters were stood behind a wall in which two slits were cut, for their guns to point through.

Shattering the stillness of the scene, a voice called through over a microphone. The voice belonged to Steven Turley, a warden at the prison who was in the room with Gardner, and he told him that he had two minutes in which he could say any last words. But Gardner responded that he had nothing to say, and even though his head remained bound, it was clear that he was trying to shake his head- no.

Turley put down the microphone, and a second later, replaced Gardner's hood. Taking the microphone with him, he left the room, leaving Gardner alone with the five gunmen who would take his life. For thirty seconds, nothing happened, and Carlisle described his nervous anticipation as he put a pair of Styrofoam plugs into his ears. It was the first execution he had ever witnessed. He had been waiting for almost a minute when he looked to the guns, and at that precise moment, they went off.

Three of the shots hit their target, landing inside the circle placed over Gardner's heart. Carlisle had expected him to die almost straight away, given what he had been told by a member of the firing squad that executed John Albert Taylor back in 1996. But Gardner didn't slump over, or go still; instead, he pushed against his restraints, clenching his fists, in what looked like pain. But without the microphone to hear Gardner crying out, and with the hood on so that his face could not be seen, it was impossible to tell.

After two minutes, Carlisle wondered whether it might have taken another volley of shots to kill him. But at that moment, a man entered the room through a side door, and smoothly and professionally checked Gardner's pulse. Finding nothing, he checked his eyes with a flashlight, and confirmed that he was dead. He was pronounced dead shortly after midnight.

A Killer Most Bizarre : The True Story of Jeremy Bamber

Joshua Cutler

Jeremy Bamber: guilty or innocent?

The nearest police car arrived at White House Farm at about 3:45am on 7 August 1985 with the call sign, Charlie Alpha 7. On the way, they had overtaken a Citroen saloon driving at 25 mph. When the officers arrived, there was no one waiting for them despite their expectations. Three or four minutes later, the Citroen pulled up and out of it came Jeremy Bamber.

Earlier that evening, Bamber has called the police explaining that his father had called him saying that "his sister has gone mental. She has a got a gun." He reported that he heard a gun-shot and the line went dead. After ringing the line a few times, it came back dead. Bamber then called the police.

The three police officers in the patrol car were Sergeant Chris Bews, PC Stephen Myall and PC Robin Saxby. Before entering the building, Bamber tells the officers that his father, mother, sister, and twin nephews were inside the farmhouse. He also several times added that his sister suffered from a psychiatric illness and that there were firearms in the house. "She is a nutter. She's been having treatment."

Bews and the other officers waited outside the White House Farm until the Essex Police Tactical Unit arrived at around 5:00am. Delaying until 7:30 am, when it was daylight, a number of loudspeaker appeals were made. No one came out. At 7:32 am, the kitchen door was broken down with a sledgehammer. Four armed officers entered the farmhouse.

Nevill Bamber, the father, lay on the kitchen floor still in his pyjamas. The kitchen has been destroyed, stools and chairs overturned, broken crockery on the floor, the lampshade of a ceiling light smashed. The telephone was found lying on the kitchen worktop, receiver off the hook.

Nevill has been shot eight times – six times in the head and neck, once in the arm and once in the shoulder. Forensics would later reveal that the head and neck shots were shot at point blank range. The arm and shoulder shots were fired from about two feet away.

In addition to his shot wounds, he had cuts, bruises, two black eyes, a fractured jaw, and a broken nose. Coupled with the kitchen being destroyed, it led to the officers believing there was some form of struggle.

Laying on the floor of the master bedroom upstairs was June, Jeremy Bamber's mother. She had been shot seven times. By following the blood splatter, she was shot once in bed and must have tried to escape, leading to a further six more shots. The shots that killed her were the ones between her eyes and the right side of her head. There were also wounds to the right side of her lower neck, her right forearm, two to the right side of her chest, and one on her right knee.

In the next bedroom lay two dead twins. Daniel was shot five times in the back of head and was still sucking his thumb when the officers found him. Nicholas, has been shot in the back of the head three times. Both twins were shot at close range.

Lastly, Shelia, the sister, was found on the floor of the master bedroom between her parents' bed and the window. Lying on top of her body was a rifle pointing towards her wounds. Her right finger lingered near the trigger. Next to her was a Bible.

When officers told Bamber what they had witnessed, he was shocked and broke down.

A detective arrived later and agreed with what his juniors told him. There was no forced sign of entry to the farmhouse. The door was closed and locked and nothing was missing.

From the get-go, the detective believed this was a murder-suicide. They accepted the report that Bamber was calm and composed throughout the scene, but failed to investigate further. Endorsing the theory that Shelia went on a fit of rage – a possibility given her character – the detective left the scene to play golf.

For some reason, the investigation became amateurish. The victims' fingerprints were not taken, nor were Bamber's. Officers collecting evidence did not wear gloves – including the .22 rifle! Two days later, feeling sorry for Bamber, they scrubbed the blood off the walls, burned the blood-stained carpets, mattresses, and bed linen on a bonfire.

According to the police, this was simple murder-suicide. However, the Bamber family was not convinced. They believed Shelia could not have killed the four members of her family. David Boutflour, who took Shelia dancing whenever he visited said "She wasn't like that. She was very gentle and beautiful".

Ann Eaton, who accompanied Bamber to the police station on the day of the killings, was also not convinced. Bamber has told the police in his statement that he had good relationships with his parents. Eaton knew this wasn't true.

In 1984, Bamber had been offered by his father to work on the farm, with the plan to eventually take it over. Within the offer was an eight percent share in the family owned caravan park with a cottage rent free, and a new car.

According to sources, Bamber reluctantly agreed to the job. He apparently hated the work and the low wage he was being paid. At the farm, other workers reported that whenever he visited the family at the farmhouse, he and his Father would argue. Bamber would go out of his way to antagonise his parents, wearing lipstick and eyeshadow, arriving late to work, and then refusing to perform tasks. This created great tension around the business.

However, it was the spring of 1985 that Bamber drew the last straw. Noticing a lack of security at the caravan park, on 23 March, he and his girlfriend, Julie Mugford, committed robbery. They stole nearly £1,000. The next day, Bamber confessed to his parents his actions, but insisted money was not the motive – giving them a lesson on how lax their security was. June, his mother, wanted him charged, but surprisingly, it was his Father who interceded and convinced June to give Jeremy a second chance.

To add fuel to the firre, Boutflour recalled a conversation about the robber. When approached by Boutlflour's father, he was asked how his conscience would allow him to kill. Bamber reply's "On no, Uncle Bobby, I could kill anybody. I could even kill my parents."

With this knowledge at hand, Boutflour and Eaton decided to search the farmhouse themselves, three days after the killings. They learned that twenty-five shots had been fired, which meant the gun had to be reloaded at least twice. Shelia, they both told later, had no basic hand-eye coordination. Apparently, "She couldn't put baked beans on toast without knocking them over".

As they searched the house, they found a silencer in the gun cupboard. Upon further inspection, they noticed the blood stain on it. After reporting these findings, it took several days before the police would collect the item for forensic examination. In addition, when the pair decided to contact the detective to explain this was not a simple murder-suicide case, their calls were refused.

For many years, the case against Bamber was dropped. They concluded that Shelia had killed her family and then herself. However, it was until 1985 when this changed. Bamber and Mugford met in London. A blazing row occurred about his involvement with another woman. Mugford's feelings changed toward Bamber and they split up.

Mugford started to tell her friends about Bamber's actual involvement in the shootings at White House Farm. Eventually, she confined the truth to the police: Jeremy Bamber had committed the murders.

His motive? Money. Having realised he overstepped the mark and fatally damaged his relationship with his parents after the robbery of the caravan park, he feared he would be removed from the will. At the time, it was believed that the property would be worth over £400,000.

Another fear that fuelled Bamber was his parents' discussion of bringing Shelia and her twin to live at the farmhouse. Playing around in Jeremy's imagination, he saw the two boys growing up on the farm, working harder than he ever did, and eventually replacing him as beneficiaries. They had to go.

Later in her statement, Mugford tells of Bamber's poor relationship with his family. He called his father "old", his mother "mad", his nephews "disturbed", and said "that his sister had nothing to live for". She also shared how Bamber planned to use Shelia as a scapegoat, using her mental health to his advantage. According to Mugford, it was his initial plan to sedate his parents and then set fire to the farmhouse. However, he skipped the idea when he discovered the contents were under-insured.

Mugford also shared telephone conversations between her and Bamber. At 9:50pm on the evening of the killings, he called to say that it was "tonight or never" and that he had been thinking about the killings all day. At 3:00am he called again: "Everything is going well. Something is wrong at the farm. I haven't had any sleep all night".

When Mugford arrived at the scene hours after the killings, apparently Bamber had told her that he had paid a man he knew, Matthew MacDonald £2,000 to perform the killings. After arresting MacDonald, it was discovered he had a strong alibi and was released without charge.

Due to Mugford's statement, Bamber was arrested on 8 September 1985. Bamber's maintained his innocence during the 5 days of questioning. His defence targeted Mugford, claiming this was a revenge act of his mishaps with other women.

On 29 September, after throughout investigation, Bamber was charged with murdering the five family members. At Maldon Magistrates' Court, it was demanded he was kept in custody.

His trial opened on 2 October 1986 by Mr. Justice Drake. The case consisted of seven men and five women. Bamber pleaded "not guilty" to the five counts of murder charged.

The Crown's opening speech focused on Bamber's motive. They claimed Bamber has seen a copy of his parents' will and was aware that with the deaths of his parents, sister, and nephews, he would inherit over £400,000.

The case lay on the murder weapon, the silencer, the telephone calls, and the finger-prints. However, the case fundamentally came down to the evidence between Bamber and Mugford.

In court, Sergeant Bews would testify that on the night of the crime, he believed that Bamber was giving too much information, too readily. He felt he was being primed as to what to expect once he went inside the farmhouse. The other police officers also commented on how calm and controlled Bamber was. "He was expecting that from the word go, wasn't he?" one of the colleagues reported.

To add to Bamber's odd behaviour, his cousins gave evidence that Jeremy was "a very, very fast driver". When asked under oath why he was driving that slow that night, despite the fears that his family may be in danger, he answered that he was driving at the speed limit.

The police admitted to overlooking vital evidence, such as not taking fingerprints, not using gloves, and burning the blood-stained furniture. Later on, the detective would receive a severe reprimand.

David Boutflour and Ann Eaton also appeared to share their investigation. They added that forensics found no traces of either lead dust from .22 bullets or gun oil from the rifle on Julie's hands or nightdress. The defence argued that Shelia could have washed and changed before finally killing herself.

Another argument bought forward by Boutflour and Eaton was related to the struggle in the kitchen. Shelia was five feet tall and weighed eight and a half stone. Nevill stood six feet four inches tall and was in good health. The probability of Shelia causing so much damage was deemed slim.

It was 9 October when Mugford was called to the stand. She recalled how about four months prior to the killings, Bamber had repeatedly shared his plans to kill his family. She was asked why she had not contacted the police earlier. She responded that she "did not want to believe what I thought. I was scared to believe it. Jeremy said that if anything happened to him, it would happen to me. He said that I would be implicated in the crime because I knew all about it."

She also provided evidence that Bamber did not call the police first after supposedly receiving the destressing phone call from his Father. According to Mugford, he called her first to tell her that "all was going well".

To further argue Bamber's guilt, PC Myall was called to stand. He was one of the first officers to arrive on the scene and spent a lot of time talking to Bamber whilst waiting for the Firearms Tactical Unit to arrive. Apparently, they talked about selling his share in the caravan park and buying a Porsche. Not the kind of conversation one would make given the situation. His actions displayed that he knew he was about to come into a lot of money, the prosecution argued. Within three weeks of the deaths, Bamber had the farmhouse valued in preparation for sale, and even took some antiques to auction.

In the closing statement, the prosecution detailed their version of the events that happened that night. After leaving the family meal at White House Farm, Bamber returned to his own home. Motivated by hatred and greed, Bamber cycled back to White House Farm in the early hours of the morning. He was careful to use the bridle path to avoid the main roads as a car would have disturbed any of his neighbours.

Bamber entered the house through the unlocked down-stairs window. He took the rifle with silencer attached and went upstairs. First, he entered his parents' bedroom and shot his mother as she was reading. She managed to get out of bed and walk a few steps before Bamber fired the fatal final shots. Next, he shot his father, but only wounded him. His father either attempted to escape or pursue Bamber downstairs into the kitchen where they both fought. Using the rifle butt, Bamber repeatedly beat his father in the face before shooting him in the head.

Bamber returned upstairs and took Shelia in to the master bedroom and shot her. Finally, whilst in their beds, the twins were shot.

The prosecution described how Bamber arranged the scene to point blame at his sister. However, when laying the rifle on top of Shelia's body, he noticed it would not fit with the silencer. As a result, he removed the silencer and hid it in the gun cupboard.

In the kitchen, Bamber dialled his own number and left the handset off the cradle. He then left the house using the kitchen window and cycled home. Not long after 3:00am, Bamber would telephone Mugford and then call the police at 3:26am.

Bamber's defence focused on Shelia's delusions, her belief of the devil and the possibility that she could have wanted to kill her parents and children. However, this was counteracted with evidence of Shelia's small stature compared to her victims.

When questioned, Bamber said that Shelia "wanted to be with God. She wanted to go heaven. She wanted to take people with her, and she wanted to save the world."

The defence concluded that no one had seen Bamber cycle from White House Farm, no cuts or bruises had been found on him to suggest a struggle, and no blood-stained clothing had been recovered.

After nineteen days of hearing arguments and evidence, the Jury retired on 27 October. For five hours, they deliberated before being sent to a hotel. The next day, the Judge called them back in to instruct them that he would accept a majority verdict. After a further nine hours, they met their verdict. With a ten-to-two majority, the foreman of the jury delivered the verdict: "Guilty". Bamber was sentenced to serve five concurrent life sentences with recommendation that he should not be released for at least twenty-five years.

Bamber still retains his innocence today, refusing to undertake offence related rehabilitation courses. This has kept him as a Category A prisoner meaning that he had "demonstrated a lack of any regard for the value of human life, and a degree of selfishness that is difficult to imagine."

During his time in prison, Bamber has tried to recover his family estate twice, failing on both accounts. However, the courts ruled both time that he should not profit from his crimes.

Bamber has since tried to appeal against his murder convictions. In November 1986, he claimed that the original judge had misdirected the jury during his summing up at the end of the trial. Apparently, the judge's language had been too forceful and against Bamber. In March 1989, the appeal was dismissed.

In 1993, Bamber petitioned the Home Secretary to have his case referred back to the Court of Appeal after the discovery of fresh evidence. It was rejected. Five months later, Bamber's twenty-five years' service was extended to a whole-life sentence.

In March 2001, the CCRC referred Bamber's case to the Court of Appeal. Sixteen issues were bought forward, fourteen were about the failures of the Essex police and two were related to the silencer and DNA testing. In December 2002, the judges dismissed appeal: "We have found no new evidence of anything that occurred which might unfairly have affected the fairness of the trial. We do not believe that the fresh evidence that has been placed before us would have had any significant impact upon the jury's conclusion if it had been available at the trial."

In May 2008, Bamber appealed at the High Court against his whole-life prison term. It was rejected. In February 2011, the CCRC refused to refer Bamber's case back to the Court of Appeal again. In

January 2012, he appealed against their sentences to the European Court of Human Rights, but once again was denied.

If Bamber was the killer, what could have led him to kill? Already it has been discussed about his greed for money, his bad relationships with his family, and the lavish life he so much desired.

It is impossible to determine if this is a genetic-triggered action. Bamber was adopted. He was born on 13 January 1961 to Juliet Wheeler, the unmarried daughter of a vicar. His father, Leslie Marsham was married and a former army sergeant. After this information was released, reporters found the biological partners and according to the reporters, the pair was unaware Bamber was their son.

Maybe his upbringing had an influence over how he led to kill. Adopted at six months old, Bamber was apparently raised in a strict and loving household. To those who knew him, he grew up to be pleasant in both attitude and appearance. He received the best possible education, attending Maldon Court prep school, then Gresham's (a boarding school). However, whilst at boarding school he was bullied for being adopted.

This could be where his resentment for his adoptive parents started. Sending him to boarding school may have triggered a thought of abandonment from his adoptive parents, just like his biological parents had done.

Bamber would walk away from boarding school with no qualifications. His father mad, Bamber went on to pass seven O-levels at sixth-form college.

His crimes allegedly started when he decided to travel the world, much to his parents' disgust. His father wanted him to work on the farm, whilst his mother wanted to impress her religious knowledge onto him. Whilst abroad, he apparently stole two expensive watches and also boasted to be involved with smuggling heroin. In addition, they had to leave New Zealand after being involved in an armed robbery. Could he have been under influence of fellow criminals or did his resentment for his adoptive parents start this series of crimes? It is hard to say, but if he did commit these crimes, something within in had changed from the pleasant boy he grew up to be.

When Bamber returned to Essex, his resentment showed. He rejected working for his father on the farm and instead took a series of low-paid menial jobs. He really didn't want to work on the farm. However, as already discussed, he eventually took a job in 1984 with eight percent share in the caravan park. From there on, as his hatred for his work developed, so did his hatred for his family. He often told Mugford that his parents were holding him back from the luxurious lifestyle he had experienced elsewhere.

Another reason for Bamber's resentment leads back to his childhood. According to Brett Collins, a close friend of Bamber's, at the age of 11, Bamber "was sexually molested by older boys and that deeply affected him." Although there are no signs of him further replicating the acts, the psychological effects could have caused him to build a further resentment to his parents for "abandoning" him to boarding school.

His defence psychiatrist performed a mental examination of Bamber. Concluding that he did actually commit the murders, supress that knowledge, and had a real belief that he did not commit the crime, which led to the diagnosis of psychopathy. "If there ever was a psychopath, it's Jeremy Bamber.

However, was this a ploy to save Bamber some years? Since being in prison, Bamber has had over 27 psychopathic tests and not one came back positive. He has also demanded lie detector tests, but they have failed to proceed.

Bamber's innocence must be considered. There are many points which could lead to his release. Firstly, the motives of David Boutflour and Ann Eaton are questioned. Unknowingly, Bamber was to inherit 50% of Boutflour and Eaton's farm. Bamber's father secretly owned this share. Not even his wife knew! More surprisingly, Eaton also owned a similar share to the caravan park as Bamber. If Bamber inherited his mother's share in the park, he would be the main shareholder, bringing in a tidy income. Could their investigation have been prompted by their dislike of Bamber?

Secondly, the timing of Bamber riding the bicycle from the White House Farm is disputed with the phone call times. It would have taken 35 minutes in the dark to ride. Given the times of the murder, he would have called from White House Farm at 3:26am to then call the police from home at 3:36am. 10 minutes in the car is acceptable, but not by bicycle.

Thirdly, according to Bamber, there was a figure in upstairs bedroom window (the light was on) when they arrived. Bamber, Bews and Myall apparently saw this. The police played it off as a trick of the light. Bews would later tell different stories to different newspapers in relation to this. It also conflicted with the story he told in court. According to newspapers, the trick of the light was the reflection of the moon, which such so happened to be rising on the other side of the house.

Finally, and quite simply, there is no forensic evidence linking Bamber to the scene of the crime. There could have been if the police actually took fingerprints and wore gloves when handling the murder weapon. However, these mistakes have been fixed with rigorous training.

This case has been a weird one. There is so much evidence against Bamber, yet the evidence defending him leaves many questions unanswered. Did he kill his parents, sister, and nephews? Was he consumed by greed for money and a luxury lifestyle? Did he really detest his parents that much?

The court considers him guilty. There is still hope and much support for Bamber and his innocence. The community are currently focused on arguing that Shelia was alive at the time the officers entered the house. With so many attempts to bring new evidence to the court rejected, their resilience and support is much to be admired.

It can be concluded that Jeremy Bamber is either the worst criminal to be incarcerated or has suffered one of the worst miscarriages of justice in recent years. Only time will tell.

THE SEX SLAVE MURDERS OF SACRAMENTO

ANA BENSON

Sacramento, California has seen a fair share of gruesome crimes during the 1970s and 1980s. That city was the hunting ground of the Original Night Stalker who is still unidentified until this day. Richard Chase was also active in the area and he was nicknamed the Vampire of Sacramento due to the uncommon ritual which included drinking the blood of his victims.

So when Gerald Gallego and his partner in crime Charlene Gallego embarked on their rampage of kidnapping and killing young teenagers, they were just a couple of many depraved criminals who were on the search for the next target around the capital of California. What made Gallego so terrifying was the fact that he had an accomplice who lured in the teenagers he had selected and the way he committed the killings by having a complete control over them.

The Gallego case once again sparked the debate about what makes a serial killer and are some people more prone to violence than the others due to their genetics?

Early life

Gerald Gallego was born in Sacramento, California on 17th July 1946. He would spend the majority of his youth in a tiny town just north of the city called Chico. His childhood wasn't easy since the environment he grew up in was quite stressful for a young boy. Gerald's mother was a sex worker while his father was constantly in and out of a jail. His mother was constantly dating abusive boyfriends who could be quite aggressive towards Gerald.

However, Gerald's father was probably the main bad influence in his life even though Gerald never actually met the man. He was a violent criminal who was incarcerated at the time of his birth. The final blow came when Gerald Gallego Sr. was arrested in Mississippi for a vehicle theft. His temper was evident to everyone because he told the authorities that he would murder the first police officer he sees after he gets out of the prison. Gallego Sr. escaped the prison in 1954 while taking a guard as his hostage. The two of them were on a run and spent a couple of days together, hiding from the police. Once Gallego Sr. was sure that the prison guard was of no use to him, he shot the man in the head, killing him on the spot.

Gallego Sr. was once again arrested and put to trial. He received a death penalty for murdering a prison guard. He was executed in 1955 in a gas chamber. Gerald Gallego was still a young boy while this was taking place. His mother made up a story about why his father is not with them but the crimes of Gallego Sr. would haunt Gerald Gallego later in his life. The children in his school and neighborhood knew the truth and weren't kind to him either, labeling Gerald as a child of a murderer.

Gerald Gallego got into crime when he was in his teens. He would often go out with his half-brother, committing petty thefts and using recreational drugs such as sniffing glue or lighter fluids. He sexually assaulted a girl who was only six years old when he was thirteen. Since he was a minor, the judge sent him to a boy's school for juvenile delinquents. Gerald and his brother escalated pretty quickly. The police tracked the brothers down after a robbery which resulted in a car chase and exchange of bullets in the middle of a street. The sentencing was light once again and he was placed in Preston School of Industry located in Ione, California. Gerald made a decision to move closer to Sacramento with his brother after his parole and they continued to steal and cheat in order to survive.

Gerald Gallego got married for the first time in 1963 when he was only sixteen. His wife was five years older than him. Just four months after the wedding, Gallego's daughter Krista was born. The marriage was a failure and the couple got divorced quickly. Gerald fought to gain the custody of his first child and the judge gave him the rights to take care of Krista. He made a decision to send the little girl to live with his mother since she didn't really fit into his lifestyle. However, he did visit the girl pretty often and it would later be discovered that he abused

Krista as well. It started when she was only six years old and would continue until the late 1970s.

Two years after the divorce, Gallego had a new bride. She was also older than him and worked as a waitress at one of Gerald's favorite bars. This woman was oblivious to Gallego's violent past so when he started physically abusing her and attacking her with pretty much anything he could find inside their home, she filed for a divorce.

It took Gallego a bit over a year to find his third wife who worked for a laundry service. Once she saw his real nature, the woman got out of the marriage as soon as possible. In 1969 Gerald was married for the fourth time to a nineteen years old girl. She also couldn't put up with the daily abuse from Gallego and asked for a divorce. She didn't know that she was pregnant with his child at the time. Gallego's second daughter was born after the divorce and she still doesn't know who her father really is.

Gerald was not giving up in his quest to find true love so he got married for the fifth time in 1974. His latest bride also worked at a laundry service and she was significantly younger than him. She did put up with his abuse for years and filed for a divorce in 1977.

In the end, Gerald was arrested for more than twenty times and he also spent some time in jail. When he was in his twenties, Gerald Gallego cleaned up his act a bit and worked as a truck driver. He later moved on to bartending. It is evident that his relationships with women were quite difficult and by the time he met his future accomplice, Gerald had seven failed marriages behind him. He would marry two of his ex-wives twice.

Meeting Charlene

Charlene Adel Williams was born in Stockton, California on 19th October 1956. Her upbringing was completely different from Gallego's because she came from a stable home with loving parents who were always there for her. She was very clever which showed in her academic records. However, Charlene did start abusing drugs and alcohol in her early twenties which led to a downfall. She was also desperate to find real love which is evident by two divorces she went through before her friends set her up with "a lovely bartender" Gerald Gallego in the summer of 1977.

The date was a success and the two became inseparable soon after. While there is no evident cause which might have prompted this good girl to trust Gallego blindly until the very end, it was clear that Charlene had a rebellious streak herself. While she might have appeared innocent to the majority of people, Charlene did experiment with various sexual fetishes which were suggested by her former husbands. Some of her friends would later say that she did it in order to keep them by her side.

Whatever the reason, Charlene was enamored with Gerald and would listen to every suggestion he made. She was ready to break every rule for him and it was clear that Gerald had found the perfect accomplice for his deviant plans.

The murders

Just one year after the first meeting between Charlene and Gerald, the two of them committed their first crime. Gerald was having personal problems at that time and he simply couldn't make love to Charlene which led him to believe that he needed an extra stimulant which would solve the issue for him. He had fantasies about having the so-called sex slaves in his home and he presented the idea to Charlene who didn't object. After all, he would abuse her every time he couldn't get an erection, putting all the blame on her. Gerald explained to Charlene that he would need to actually hunt down a female and capture her before locking her up and using her for his own pleasure.

While Charlene was a bit confused by this, she was still on board even though she wasn't certain about her own role in the process. Everything will be revealed to her after the couple drove to a mall in Sacramento and parked their vehicle in an adjacent parking lot. Gerald instructed her to go out and find a teenage girl who would fit his sex slave fantasies. Charlene bumped into Rhonda Scheffler and Kippi Vaught who were sixteen and seventeen at the time. She told them that there was some weed back in her Dodge van and invited the girls to come along and get high together. They agreed and followed Charlene back to the vehicle where Gerald was waiting.

Once Charlene opened a door, Gerald pointed his gun at the girls, commanding them to come inside which they did. He quickly tied their hands and legs. Charlene drove the van to Baxter, California which is a remote place near Sierra Nevada mountain range. Gerald sexually assaulted both girls and then shot each of them in the head. The mere act of tying the girls and making the other watch the rape of her friend tells a lot about the sadistic personality Gerald had. It is also clear that the girls were hit with a heavy object before the fatal shots. They left them in a ditch without even trying to conceal the bodies. Their lifeless corpses would be found two days later.

Two weeks after the first murders, Gerald's daughter Krista visited the police station in Sacramento. It took her years of torture to finally put an end to the sexual abuse she endured from her father. Krista accused Gerald Gallego of sodomy, incest, and unlawful sexual intercourse. Gallego wasn't ready to face the authorities now when he just started turning his deviant fantasies into reality so he told Charlene that they would be moving away.

The cooling off period lasted for less than a year. Charlene and Gerald got married in the meantime and moved to Houston, Texas. They used aliases and would often travel to Reno, Nevada. That is where the second set of murders occurred in June of 1979. The newlyweds were driving around Washoe County Fair which is pretty close to Reno. The modus operandi was almost similar to the first two murders where Charlene was supposed to talk the girls into coming to her van. Since she was a young woman, the victims felt safe around her without sensing any impending danger.

Charlene started talking to Brenda Judd and Sandra Colley who were thirteen and fourteen at the time of their abduction. They agreed to go to Charlene's van where Gerald greeted them with a pointed gun and told the girls to get into the van. Charlene was once again the chauffeur while Gerald raped the girls in the back of the vehicle. The assaults lasted for about two hours and once Gerald was done, Charlene parked the car and watched him drag the girls out. Gerald then bludgeoned the girls with a hammer proving once again that he enjoyed the power he had over his victims.

Since they were left on a desolate road somewhere in Nevada, the law enforcement didn't find their bodies for decades. Brenda Judd and Sandra Colley were considered missing at the time and the police didn't start a murder investigation in this case right away.

The third set of murders also occurred one year later. The Gallegos followed the same pattern as in the first abduction by choosing the victims in a mall. They were once again back in Sacramento. Stacy Ann Redican and Karen Chipman-Twiggs were in a bookstore that day and after Gerald picked them out from the crowd, Charlene approached them. The girls followed her to the van and were made to come inside by Gerald. Charlene was in the driver's seat, occasionally glancing back to see what Gerald was doing to the girls. He ordered the girls to get undressed which they did. Gerald needed the control over the girls because he loved the feeling of being commanding and supreme. Both Stacy Ann and Karen were brutally raped and then murder by a blunt force trauma to their heads. The police would uncover their bodies three months later in July of 1980.

Their seventh victim was Linda Teresa Aguilar who was hitchhiking alone on 6th June 1980 in Oregon. Linda was four months pregnant at the time of the abduction. The couple picked her up promising that they would drive her to wherever she was going to and Gerald sexually assaulted her soon after. Linda's body was discovered more than two weeks after the murder. The investigators noticed that she had head injuries and they also found traces of bonds on her wrists and ankles. It was evident that she was beaten with a rock and then strangled. Her body was buried so the most shocking evidence was the fact that Linda had sand in her nose and lungs which indicated that she was still alive as Gerald placed her in the shallow grave near Gold Beach.

The next murder happened on Gerald's birthday in 1980. This was the first time Gerald selected a woman he knew so the pattern of the killings did change a bit. Virginia Mochel was a bartender in a place which was frequently visited by Gerald and Charlene in West Sacramento. Virginia was abducted from a parking lot after she completed her shift. The woman was dragged into Gallego's van where he proceeded to violently rape her. She was so tired of everything he had done to her over the course of several hours that she ended up begging Gerald to kill her and end her suffering. He strangled Virginia Mochel and dumped her corpse near a pond in Clarksburg, California. She would be discovered by a couple of fishermen three months after the murder. Even though her body was almost completely decomposed, the investigators found traces of the fishing line which was used to subdue her. The cord was still around her neck which confirmed the suspicion that she was strangled.

Craig Miller and Mary Elizabeth Sowers were the last victims of Gerald and Charlene. On 2nd November 1980, Miller and Sowers were leaving a party and were standing by a road when a car parked in front of them. This was the first time that Gerald Gallego actually exited the vehicle first and pointed his gun at this young couple. He ordered them to get inside but luckily, their friend Andy who was nearby managed to write down the license plates which would be the key evidence in stopping this murderous duo. As he approached the car to see what was going on, Charlene jumped out and told him to go away. She was once again driving the vehicle and as soon as they got to a remote and dark place, Gerald ordered Craig to get out of the car.

He obliged and Gerald shot him in the back of his head, killing him instantly. He didn't even bother to cover up the body and the car drove off. Charlene was ordered to go back to their apartment with Mary Elizabeth and they took her inside where Gerald proceeded to rape the girl. The assault lasted for hours and once Gerald was done, all three of them got back into the vehicle. They once again arrived at another secluded area where Gerald shot Mary Elizabeth.

The investigation and the arrest

Andy who was a friend of Craig Miller and Mary Elizabeth Sowers waited for the morning in order to see if they came home safely. When he found out the couple was missing, Andy contacted the local law enforcement describing everything he saw that night – two people in a vehicle who drove Miller and Sowers away. He also gave the license plate number to the police who began their investigation right away.

The plate number led the investigators to the address of Charlene Gallego's parents who told them that their daughter was using their car. The police were confused by their findings because Charlene's parents were upstanding citizens so they thought they got the wrong information. But they proceeded to question Charlene who denied having any connection to the abduction of the young sweethearts. However, when they dug deeper into her life, they discovered that her husband did have a criminal past. The pieces started to connect and the investigators got a search warrant for their house and vehicle.

Charlene agreed to give the keys of the car to the investigator who was on the scene and she behaved politely. Gerald was nowhere to be seen at the time. The investigator entered the vehicle but couldn't find a thing that would indicate foul play. Charlene was pregnant at the time so she excused herself by saying she had morning sickness. The detectives agreed and asked her to come back to the station when she feels better in order to continue her interview.

Since there were no bodies, the police still approached this as a missing person case. However, Charlene didn't arrive at the station for an interview so Gene Burchett who was a homicide detective at the time went back to the house of Charlene's parents to see if she was around. He was talking to them when he got the call about a discovery of a corpse. Burchett drove straight to the scene of the crime where he found Craig Miller's lifeless body. He realized that this case is way bigger than they initially though, especially now when Charlene was not at home and Mary Beth was still missing.

The detectives found Gerald's address and tried to track them down there but no one was home. They would soon find out that Gerald and Charlene were on the run because they knew that the police was after them. The investigators entered the apartment and found numerous guns and firearm neatly displayed all over the tables. There was a lot of ammunition laying around as well but they couldn't connect it to the murder of Craig Miller.

However, a fellow bartender who worked with Gerald Gallego called the police and told them that Gerald did shoot his gun inside the bar one night. The officers arrived at the scene and collected the bullet which linked Gerald's gun to the bullets found at the scene of Craig Miller's murder. They were now certain that Gallego was the one who killed the young student. But they still needed to track him down.

It appeared that the murderous couple was on the run from the police but they were running low on money. Charlene contacted her parents from Salt Lake City asking them to send her some funds through a bank. They did so without contacting the law enforcement so the couple continued to travel from one city to another. They were first in Denver, Colorado but soon relocated to Omaha, Nebraska. The Gallegos were once again broke so Charlene called her parents. They realized the severity of the crimes their daughter was involved in so they told the FBI everything they knew. FBI waited for Gerald and Charlene at the Western Union bank in Omaha because they knew they would pick up the money there. And sure enough, the Gallegos entered the building as scheduled. They were arrested without any fight. Both of them were transferred to California where preparations for a trial were under way. Since Charlene was pregnant she gave birth to Gerald Gallego's first son while in prison. Charlene's parents got the custody of Gerald Armond Gallego Jr.

The trials

The law enforcement knew that the Gallegos were probably guilty for more than two murders so they focused on Charlene during the interrogations. The detectives were pretty sure that she was the weaker link and that making Gerald Gallego talk would be almost impossible. After hours and hours of questions, Charlene made a deal with the police, agreeing to tell them all and also to testify against Gerald in his trial for a lesser sentence. Two trials were scheduled – one in California and one in Nevada. Nebraska refused to file any charges against the couple so there wasn't a third trial.

Charlene pleaded guilty to the murders of Craig Miller and Mary Elizabeth Sowers so she received a minimal sentencing of sixteen years and eight months. It is the lowest punishment for a first-degree murder in California state and the prosecutor wasn't happy with the end result but he understood the importance of getting the whole story, as well as having a very important witness to tell every single detail once Gerald's trial comes around. Charlene made the similar deal with the judge in Nevada, once again getting the lowest punishment. Everything was ready for the main trial because it was Gerald Gallego's turn to appear in the courtroom.

Showing his true narcissistic traits, Gerald Gallego refused the court appointed defense. Instead, he acted as his own lawyer, making numerous mistakes during the process. He failed to cross-examine many important witnesses while focusing solely on Charlene whom he questioned for nearly a week. From the very start, Charlene claimed that she was afraid of Gerald who would often physically abuse her. She said that she was almost his hostage because he had a full control of her bank account and she simply couldn't get away from their toxic relationship. Gerald would often blame her for everything he was doing to the other girls.

Charlene told the jury: "I tried to get away. I tried, and people, especially women, will say, 'well, if you want to get away you can always get away.' It's not that easy; it's not that easy at all. I don't know why Gallego didn't kill me because he sure tried."

On the other hand, Gerald told the courtroom that Charlene was more than willing to help him out with the killings. As a matter of fact, she was an active participant in the assaults as well. Gerald also accused Charlene of putting the entire blame on him in order to save herself. As the trial was nearing the end, Gerald took the stand which allowed the prosecution to ask him questions, debunking many of his claims. On 21st of June 1983, Gerald Gallego received a death penalty in California for the murders of Craig Miller and Mary Elizabeth Sowers.

Now it was time to transfer him to Nevada and arrange a new trial for him over there. Gallego was accused of murdering Stacy Redican, Karen Twiggs, Brenda Judd and Sandra Colley in the state of Nevada. Despite the efforts of the local police enforcement, the bodies of Brenda Judd and Sandra Colley weren't found at the time. Charlene did provide the investigators with everything she knew about the location where they left the girls but she wasn't one hundred percent sure because the place itself was pretty desolate.

However, Charlene told the investigators to compare the rope from Gerald's car to the one which was used to bound Stacy Redican and Karen Twiggs. It was a perfect match and when combined with Charlene's testimony, the prosecution had a solid case against Gerald Gallego. He did make an important change for this trial and allowed Gary Marr to be his defense lawyer. They continued the same narrative as in California claiming that Charlene was trying to save herself by providing the courtroom with false testimony.

The jury found him guilty in just a little bit over two hours of deliberation. Gerald Gallego received yet another death penalty but this time it was in Nevada.

The aftermath

Gerald Gallego continued to say that he was innocent throughout the years of his incarceration. He did file a couple of appeals in which he protested his representation in court. Nevada Supreme Court allowed him a new hearing in 1999 and he once again received a death penalty. Gallego was held in Ely State Prison, Nevada up until his death on 18th July 2002. He died of rectal cancer which was untreated and managed to spread to his lungs and liver. He was moved to prison's medical center. Gallego was in terrible pain a couple of weeks before his death and spent his last moments under heavy medication.

Charlene Gallego became Charlene Williams in 1985 when she divorced from Gerald. She served her sentence and was released from Nevada prison in the summer of 1997. She moved away from the West Coast, leaving her parents in California. Even though she didn't say where she was going, Charlene promised to register herself as a felon wherever she settled down. It would be discovered in 2013 that she changed her name and was back in California with her new husband.

KILLER SEDUCTRESS

GARY RACE

Shayna Hubers

Shayna Hubers is a 21-year-old graduate from Lexington, Kentucky. She grew up in a comfortably middle-class family and was a smart young woman. She graduated from Paul Laurence Dunbar High School in 2009, and went on to college. During high school, Shayna's friends described her as quiet and "most likely to succeed". Shayna graduated from Kentucky's prestigious School of the Arts after making Dean's list in 2012. She was in the process of pursuing a Master's Degree in counseling from Eastern Kentucky University when she took the life of her on-again off-again boyfriend, Ryan Poston and effectively put her life on hold.

Poston was a 29-year-old lawyer and business owner from a successful family of attorneys and executives. He was loved by his friends and family and admired by women. He was known to be friendly, respectful and respectable, and an overall good guy. He met Hubers in 2011 through mutual friends on Facebook and the attraction was instantaneous, as the first photos of Hubers that Poston saw were racy in nature. The two began to chat, and started officially dating shortly after they went on their first date. They continued their relationship for over a year. If it hadn't been for Facebook, the two more than likely never would have met, as Shayna lived 80 miles away from Ryan and had no reason to venture into Ryan's neck of the woods.

Throughout the entirety of the relationship, the couple sent thousands of text messages, including a conversation about possibly taking a two-week long break from each other and the relationship. Hubers was also known to post pictures of herself and Poston on Instagram. The seemingly happy couple exchanged over a thousand photo messages, as well as 20,000 messages through Facebook. Most of the Facebook messages had been sent by Hubers to Poston, who had responded to only a handful of them.

To people who weren't aware of the couple's dynamics, it appeared as if they were a happy couple who had everything going for them.

They were both beautiful, successful, and driven. It was a match made in heaven- or so it appeared to be, but the truth was much darker and would become the subject of a complicated trial and a life term in prison.

On October 11, 2012, Hubers and Poston and his family had dinner at the young lawyer's home. After dinner, Hubers went home- she returned a few hours later, however, and the couple got into a heated argument. Poston informed his girlfriend that he wanted to end their 18-month long relationship, and it set Hubers off into a fit of anger. Her anger worsened when she was later told that Poston already had a date lined up with the 2012 Miss Ohio, Audrey Bolte. It's believed that the news of Ryan's new date was what pushed Hubers over the edge.

In the morning, Hubers' mother drove two hours to pick up her daughter and the two went out shopping. They were out for most of the day before Shayna was dropped back off at Ryan's house, telling her mother that she wanted to stay with him. Despite her other asking her numerous times to come home with her, Hubers was adamant that she wanted to stay at Poston's house. Shortly after, Poston became aware that Shayna was planning to stay at his place- he used this time to inform her that he had another date and didn't intend to spend the night with her. By 9 o'clock that night, the young lawyer was dead on his dining room floor.

At 8:53 that chilly Friday night, Hubers placed a 911 call from Poston's condo and said to the responding dispatcher: "Ma'am, I have…I have…I have killed my boyfriend in self-defense".

The dispatcher then asked what happened, to which Hubers replied "He beat me and tried to carry me out of the house and I came back in to get my stuff. He was right in front of me and reached down to grab the gun. I grabbed it out of his hands and pulled the trigger".

The dispatcher then instructed Hubers to step outside with her hands in front of her. Hubers complied, and responding officer, David

Fornash's partner cuffed and took her away while Fornash himself went to investigate the crime scene.

Fornash and the other officers who responded to the scene, found Ryan Poston lying on his dining room floor next to a Sig Sauer .380-caliber pistol. The pistol, upon further inspection, was found to have belonged to Poston, who had a passion for guns. "...he would have them in his boot, he would have them in his holster..." says Poston's ex-girlfriend, Lauren Whorley, who claimed that Poston's love of guns made her feel safe.

Fornash went room to room, double checking that there were no other hiding in the apartment and upon finding Poston's body, officers found that he had been shot once in the back, twice in the head, and three times in his upper body. The coroner is called and Fornash sets off for the station where Hubers had been escorted into an interrogation room and sat waiting.

Meanwhile Poston, lying dead on his kitchen floor, was supposed to meet with Audrey Bolte at the Milford Inn bar for a night of drinks and harmless flirting. Poston, however, did not show up and Bolte went home feeling confused. When asked how she felt about him not showing up, Bolte said that it was odd for Poston not to show up or give some sort of notice that he wasn't coming, as he was a very responsible individual.

Friends of Poston claim that he and Hubers were never really in a committed relationship, as Poston lost interest in Hubers rather quickly and made several halfhearted attempts to break it off with her. In fact, by October of 2012, Ryan had made 3 attempts to sever Shayna's ties to him. According to text messages between Poston and his cousin, he was emotionally drained from dealing with Shayna. "I received 75 text messages from her. I am emotionally and mentally spent. I hope she leaves me alone" reads one message between the cousins. Despite this, Poston continued to go out with Hubers and pose for photos.

Shayna, confiding in a friend through text messages, said that Poston had told her that he's only with her because he felt bad when she cries. She is also quoted as saying: "My love has turned to hate."

In one particularly chilling message Shayna claims that "...tonight when I go to the shooting range with Ryan, I want to turn around, shoot, and kill him, and play like it's an accident." The next day, Shayna posts a photo of herself with a gun at the shooting range.

The night of the murder, Shayna was interviewed about the incident. Left alone in the interogation room, Shayne almost seemed proud of what she had done, reports Chief Bill Birkenhauer. He watched her on live camera snapping her fingers, dancing around, and muttering to herself "I killed him, I killed him."

Legally, officers were not allowed to interrogate her without an attorney present, so when she was brought into the interview room they didn't ask any questions. In fact, officers didn't say anything. Shayna, however, readily volunteered her story of how the events took place. She was rambling on for two hours before running out of things to say. According to officers, the men and women who took turns sitting with Shayna, quickly grew tired of her rambling and would have preferred to leave. "Shayna appeared to be nervous, or trying to cover something up" one officer said. "...her stories, after a while, stopped matching up and kept changing." This, according to the officer, might have been happening as a result of Shayna realizing that she was in over her head.

When speaking about Poston's death, Hubers said that she knew he was dead because he was twitching. Her exact words were: "Literally, that's when I knew that he was dead or close to it...the twitching...and that was it." She goes on to explain how she couldn't let him sit there and twitch. She couldn't stand to sit there and watch him die so she shot 5 more rounds into his body to finish him off.

In addition to building a case of self-defense and trying to convince officers that she deeply loved Ryan, she claims that "he was very vain...he wants to get a nose job...I shot him right here-" she pointed to her nose and continued her story "...and I gave him the nose job that he wanted."

Officers didn't buy Shayna's claims of self defense due to lack of evidence that Poston was ever abusive towards her. "She claimed that she was pushed and that he hit her, however, there were no visible marks or wounds at all on any part of Shayna's body" says former FBI profiler James Fitzgerald.

"There was no evidence in Ryan's condo that there was a fight" adds Laura Richards, a prominent criminal behavioral analyst.

Photos from the crime scene show evidence against Shayna's claims of a fight, as there were a number of pill bottles and bullets standing on end on the table. Had a fight taken place, they would have been knocked over or displaced and the murder area would have been left a mess. Instead, it was neat and tidy other than the pool of Ryan's blood that was left behind after the shooting. Shayna had also claimed that Poston had thrown her against a bookshelf. The bookshelf in question, when police arrived, was undisturbed.

As for Shayna's odd behavior when left alone, Richards believes that it was an act in an attempt to appear mentally unstable and open the door for the insanity plea should her self-defense claims fall short. "She couldn't decide which plea to go with- self-defense or insanity. So, she decided to open the doors to both and see which one panned out the best."

After three hours of deliberation, Shayna is charged with one count of first degree murder. In 2014, her trial is well underway and a forensic pathologist mentions that at the time he was shot, Poston had been sitting down- a fact that goes against what Shayna had said previously. According to Richards, this fact alone blows Shayna's claims of self-defense out the window as it shows that Ryan was not charging at her in a fit of rage, as she had previously claimed. Instead, he had been seated and had been seated great distance away from Shayna at the time of the murder. Forensic expert Howard Ryan backs this theory up by going into detail about the shots that Shayna fired at Poston. He says that the first shot was to Poston's head, a fact that is significant due to the lack of blood found on Ryan's shirt.

"If he had been standing up, the gravity would have brought it down...straight down the shirt through the bottom to the pants" he says.

Using the blood stains on the table, Ryan is able to provide further detail as to why he believes that Poston was sitting down. "When she shoots him in the forehead, his head goes down on the table." Poston's head would not have fallen onto the table if he had been in an upright position. From here, Ryan suspects that Poston's back was left exposed, setting him up for the next shot. At the same time that he is being shot a second time, his right arms falls limp and opens up the area of his body that will receive the third shot- which is right underneath of his arm. After this, his body slumps to the floor and remains there until it is removed by the coroner.

Three of Shayna's cellmates testified against her that day, claiming that she had told them that she intended to kill Ryan that night and that he had never been abusive to her. "She laughed about shooting him in the face and giving him the nose job he always wanted" claims Cecily Miller.

Another inmate, Holly Nivens, claims that Shayna made the whole abuse story up. When speaking about the bruises and scratches that Shayna would show people, Nivens claimed that Shayna inflicted them on herself.

Shayna also told her cellmates that she had messed the apartment up and thrown objects around to make it appear as though a vicious fight had taken place.

Shayna didn't take the stand, but prosecutors used her social media and interview footage as a substitution. Despite the overwhelming evidence against Hubers, her defense team maintained its argument that Poston had been abusive and that Shayna had acted out of self defense when she shot him.

A toxicologist was asked to plead in Shayna's defense and said that at the time of his death, Ryan had a strong mix of Xanax and Adderall in his system. He argues that these medications could have caused outbursts of anger and violence, making it possible for Ryan to snap and come after Hubers with a both his fists and then later on, a deadly weapon such as a gun.

A clinical psychologist was also called to testify on her behalf, and he diagnosed her with bipolar disorder with narcissistic tenancies, and post traumatic stress disorder (PTSD).

"She was very distraught. She was depressed" says the psychologist who claims that Shayna had told him that she had suffered from sexual abuse as a child, and was recognized as having alcohol and prescription drug abuse issues.

On the day of the trial, Shayna painted herself as a model girl friend to Poston, claiming that he had been going through a lot and that she had always been there for moral support.

"I was always good to him" she said.

Again, the jury didn't buy the story. Five hours after her trial started, Shayna was officially charged. She appeared back in court three months later for sentencing and was given 40 years behind bars. Shayna's defense team tried to lower the time before she becomes eligible for parole to 8 years instead of 20, but was denied this motion.

Just six months later, her legal team filed another motion seeking a new trial. According to her team, one of the jurors who convicted Shayna had not been legally eligible to convict her as he was a convicted felon himself. This, according to Kentucky law, made him unable to serve the court and gave Shayna's legal team a reason for a new trial.

It's said that Shayna's new trial date is set for early 2018. Until then, she is behind bars and serving her 40 year sentence as planned.

The new trial was originally set for January of 2018, but has been put on hold for 4 months longer at the request of Shayna's legal team. The extra time, according to her attorney, will be used to prepare.

Despite the 40 year sentence, Ryan's friends and loved ones are left with a sour taste in their mouths. Lauren Whorley, in an interview with a news station, claims that she wishes she would have known what was going on- maybe then she would have been able to help and prevent Ryan from getting too tangled up in Hubers. She also said that she believes the trial should have been handled in an "an eye for an eye" fashion, meaning that what Shayna did to Ryan, should have been done back to her as justice.

"Maybe it's traditional, old-school mentality, but if you kill someone, then you know, it's an eye for an eye. And what you due unto others should be done unto you" she said.

For her, however, the sentencing brought a sliver of much appreciated peace. "I was there when they read it" she said about the final verdict "It was the longest 30 seconds of my life."

Matt Herren, a close friend of Ryan, still struggles to make sense of what went wrong that night. "I think about him everyday," he says "You just don't think something like that will happen to someone you know."

Like Whorley, Matt wonders if there is something he could have done to prevent Ryan from suffering the fate he did. "I know a lot of people in his life feel the same way" he says to "48 Hours" correspondent Peter Van Sant.

Van Sant asked Herren what was lost when Ryan was killed and Herren responded with "He's the type of person you want in your life. Not just a friend, but a loving son, a protective, older brother. He had three younger sisters that he adored." Poston had cared deeply for his three younger sisters and only ever wanted the best for them. In return, they showered him with love and looked up to their older brother.

Ryan and his family had been close-knit, despite his mom and dad divorcing when he was a child. He was close to his father, and when his mother remarried, he grew an attachment to his new step-father, Peter Carter. Ryan thought of him as a second father.

According to Sarah Robinson, a woman who had grown up with Shayna, her future had seemed promising as well. Shayna had been a good student and was never in any trouble.

"I thought she was, close to genius, in my opinion" she said " I mean, she was always in AP classes. Always getting A's in everything."

During her academic career, Hubers had received various awards for academic excellence and leadership.

"She liked to succeed at anything and everything she did" Robinson concludes.

When Van Sant asked her what Shayna had been like with boys in high school, Robinson mentioned that Shayna could be dramatic. "If a guy, broke up with her or something, she would take it pretty hard" she explained "...crying, and a maybe a bit of screaming..she didn't really like to let things go."

When asked if Shayna had been happy with Ryan, Robinson said that as far as she knew, she had been. As far as she knew, they had both been happy.

Ryan's friend, Allie Wagner, claimed that there was something wrong with the relationship from the start when she was asked the same question about Ryan. According to Wagner, Shayna had been cold upon their first meeting. "You could just immediately tell that...that she was obsessed with him," she says.

"He was busy with work..he didn't really have time for anyone" Herren adds. "He didn't want to hurt her feelings..that wasn't the kind of person he was."

As Shayna's denial towards Ryan's disinterest progressed, he started to wonder if he might need to put a restraining order out against her. "This is getting to be restraining order level crazy..." he wrote in a text message to his cousin "She's shown up at my condo 3 times and refuses to leave each time."

Ryan's neighbor, Nikki Carnes claims that there may have been two sides to the tumultuous relationship. She says that Ryan may have been emotionally abusive. According to Carnes, Shayna complained frequently of Ryan putting her down. "She told me that he would say she needed a boob job or a face lift and that she was fat and needed to lose some weight" she says.

Van Sant then asked her why Shayna wouldn't have left and she replied "I guess because she was young and she always told me she loved him." Carnes also told Van Sant that Shayna did everything for Ryan from taking his dog outside to picking up and doing his laundry. On the night of the shooting, she also reportedly heard gunshots but didn't hear the couple fighting, as Shayna had claimed that they had.

Wagner, when asked what she thought could have happened that night replied, "I think she went over there...tried to talk him out of breaking up with her. And I think he just stood his ground for the first time," she said "I think he just said no, like, this isn't working. So she picked up the gun and shot him."

Chief Birkenhauer agreed with Wagner's theory "He wanted to break up with her...I think that Shayna was not gonna be broken up with" he said in an interview with Van Sant.

Prosecutor Michelle Snodgrass explains why Shayna's pleas of abuse were dismissed. "Someone who is in shock does not pirouette," she says in response to the police videos of Shayna singing and dancing in the interview room "Within hours of putting six bullets in Ryan Poston and watching him die, she was dancing and singing."

"There were hundreds of thousands of text messages. And most of them were from Shayna. For every 1 message Ryan sent, she sent probably 50," Snodgrass says "She couldn't stop herself."

According to Snodgrass, rejection was what ultimately pushed Shayna over the edge and drove her to kill the man she so desperately loved.

"Ryan's a bright guy; he's a lawyer" says Van Sant to Snodgrass "Why wouldn't he get a restraining order?"

"Under the law in Kentucky, he didn't qualify for a restraining order. The law in Kentucky required the two to have been living together or to have been married" she replied.

Van Sant then spoke to Hubers' mother, Sharon, about the tragedy. "She graduated cum laude in three years at the University of Kentucky. She was pursuing a Master's Degree in school guidance counseling," she said.

"And what do you want people to know after reading this" Van Sant asked "...in relation to this case?"

"Shayna Hubers is not a child, a girl, a person that would murder someone; that would wake up and say 'OK, I'm going to shoot somebody"

"I want the world to know who Shayna is. And I want them to hear it from her mother" she concludes tearfully.

Hubers and her mother had been close most of Shayna's life, according to Sarah Robinson. "I think she was very close to her mom. I think her mom, for a good portion of her life, could have been her best friend."

This statement is backed up by a quote from Sharon Hubers in her interview with Van Sant: "That child has been a blessing to me. She's my whole life."

"The word that has been used to describe your daughter is evil" Van Sant teold Sharon.

"She's far from evil. Shayna has a heart of gold. She's like her mommy...a loving spirit. That's what I want the world to know" she replied.

After the trial, Shayna spoke up for the first time. Despite having killed their beloved family member, she didn't apologize to Poston's family. Instead, she apologized to her family and friends, and speaks only of herself.

"I'm sorry to my family. And I'm sorry to my friends for letting them down. And I'm sorry for the money my parents had to spend on attorneys" she says, after being convicted of the murder.

"I do wanna help people. I do wanna be something better. And I do want to continue to grow and learn" she said to the judge "And I just don't think a 40 year sentence will help me. I don't think it would benefit me any."

Judge Fred Stine replied to Shayna's statement with his own choice words. "What I think happened in that apartment was little more than cold-blooded murder."

Regardless of what happened that night, a promising young lawyer lays dead, and a successful college student sits rotting behind bars. Two families have been destroyed, and law officials are left baffled. Both the victim and offender have been robbed of their lives- and for what? For a reason that the offender calls love.